DAY BY DAY

DAY BY DAY

Six months' devotional readings
by Wong Ming-Dao

HIGHLAND BOOKS

Printed in Great Britain for
HIGHLAND BOOKS
Broadway House, The Broadway,
Crowborough, East Sussex, TN6 1HQ
by Richard Clay Ltd, Bungay, Suffolk.
Typeset by Rowland Phototypesetting Ltd,
Bury St Edmunds, Suffolk

From the Chinese Publisher's Introduction

From the regular preaching of Mr Wong Ming-Dao and from his writings which are spread over thirty years, we may discern some outstanding elements. He distinguished between the true gospel and the counterfeit gospel; sounded a warning against all traditions and customs in the church that did not harmonise with the truth; rebuked worldliness, apostasy and all manifestations of corruption and sinfulness; and emphasised the need for believers to live devout and holy lives.

Much of what Mr Wong wrote and preached, other preachers were unwilling or afraid to preach. Yet such teaching is needed more than ever today amid all the adverse currents generated by the mixing of worldly customs with the life of the church.

Throughout his life, Mr Wong has without question carried out faithfully the task that God entrusted to him and has indeed been true to his own vows. Arising from this, he won the love and respect of uncounted believers but, at the same time, brought upon himself the jealous hatred, opposition and vilification of many other people – in particular of a number who were in positions of church leadership. This hostility became so fierce on the part of some, that they influenced people in authority and thus became the instruments through whom Mr Wong suffered harm and persecution. By acting in this way, these people exposed the bitter malice that they had allowed to take root in their own hearts.

Although this opposition persisted over a period of several decades, Mr Wong never wavered in his determination to be faithful to the Lord 'unto death.' He always set himself to expound truth and to unmask error. He is well qualified to declare: 'I have fought the good fight, I have finished the race, I have kept the faith. Now there is in store for me the crown of righteousness.'

The English Translator's Foreword

The ability of Chinese Christians to maintain their witness, as they have done throughout recent decades of pressure, is undoubtedly due — at least in part — to the faithfulness, tenacity and courage, as well as the gifts of outstanding evangelical leaders. Among these, if we are thinking of an all-round ministry, it is difficult not to regard Wong Ming-Dao as one of God's greatest gifts to the Christians of China.

Wong Ming-Dao never completed a university course, never travelled abroad except to places like Hong Kong and Macao, and lacked many of the educational opportunities enjoyed by others. He realised that academic qualifications do not constitute the major element in the foundations for Christian ministry. Once he had the prospect of being supported by a mission organisation not only to take a university course in China but also to pursue theological studies in the United Kingdom, but he forfeited these opportunities, through refusing to compromise in matters on which he held strong convictions. This trait of unwillingness to compromise, even when his own interests were at stake, was undoubtedly one of the secrets of his strong leadership.

At the time of writing (1989) Mr Wong is eighty-nine and living in retirement with his wife in Shanghai. They have one son. In his fifties Mr Wong was among the preachers sent to prison by those in authority. He was in prison for twenty-three years and his wife for twenty years. He was released in

1980 at the age of eighty. Considering the years in which he was denied public ministry, it is as if he died in his prime. But he packed an enormous amount of work into the years when he was healthy and free to move around. He was aware that he needed to work while it was day. Yet he emphasised that Christian workers must always operate within the will of God and as God directs. Although he exerted a tremendous influence on evangelical Christians in China, his leadership did not give rise to a new denomination.

Wong Ming-Dao's ministry was three-fold. First, he was the overseer of a large congregation in Peking (though he would never make use of any status-giving title). The work that he directed had been built up over many years.

It began in a small way. Having ceased to work as a young teacher in a mission school in Baoding, the provincial capital of Hobei, he returned to Peking where he joined a Pentecostal meeting under the leadership of Teacher Ju who had baptised him. But he was unhappy about some of the features that characterised this particular assembly and he consequently left them. But he did not attach himself to any other group. He gave himself to diligent Bible study in his own home, and he was presently joined by other believers to whom he ministered. From these small beginnings the work gradually developed, as related in his autobiographical writings, *A Stone Made Smooth* (Mayflower Christian Books). The growing congregation rented various premises in turn, but eventually erected their own meeting place – The Christians' Tabernacle.

His second sphere of ministry was that of special speaker at evangelistic meetings and at conventions for believers in cities all over China. The time came, in fact, when he would spend six months in the year – though not consecutively – in this wider ministry.

His third regular ministry was his literary work. He began this ministry in the 1920s by publishing four booklets. Not long afterwards, he began to edit and publish a regular magazine called *Spiritual Food Quarterly*. He had to decline a request to publish the magazine monthly because he himself was responsible for most of the contents. Since the messages of these publications are essentially biblical they are not only apposite in any generation but they also apply as much in the West as in the East. They can thus be appreciated in translation, as in this present volume.

The story of Mr Wong's struggle against the military edicts in Peking, at the time of the occupation, is told elsewhere. It must be pointed out, however, that his resistance was not on political grounds. The instructions issued by the authorities required him and his church to join a federation dominated by churches that were theologically liberal (what he called 'unbelieving churches'). Although his refusal to join such an ecumenical organisation entailed the risk of imprisonment or worse, he did not give way, so strongly did he feel that this would be an act of disobedience and disloyalty to God.

In the event, the Japanese authorities never arrested him. But a few years later, when an unsympathetic Chinese government made similar demands, the consequences of his courageous stand for the faith was a long term of imprisonment. Yet nothing comes out more clearly in his writings than the firm conviction that nothing untoward can befall the faithful servant of God unless God himself permits it.

Two themes predominated in his messages. He consistently emphasised the importance of maintaining a high standard of Christian life, while denouncing sinful practices in the lives of believers and churches. Secondly, he emphasised matters of faith. Along with expositions of basic doctrines, he did not hesitate to issue warnings against false teachers and against leaders who were theologically liberal. He never wished or sought to be controversial in his ministry, but the role of contender for the faith was thrust upon him by contemporary tendencies and practices.

From first to last Wong Ming-Dao had the unwavering support of a like-minded wife who stood by him in all the hard decisions that he was compelled to make and in all the hard experiences through which he had to pass.

Mr Wong was not of course free from either shortcomings or failures. When he and his wife gained early release from their imprisonment by signing a confession, they came to see this as dishonouring to God and gave themselves up again. And that was the beginning of their long imprisonment. Mr Wong acknowledged that he had acted like Peter. But never was he a Judas.

For myself I can still hear in memory the ringing tones of Mr Wong's voice, in a large and packed auditorium in Nanking, as he fervently expounded the doctrine of the bodily resurrection of Christ. We can only salute this fine and fearless warrior, and seek grace from God to follow his example of steadfastness, courage and obedience. And as we read these messages, we cannot do other than bear in mind that the writer is one who, with his wife, has long been tempered in the fires of suffering.

Arthur Reynolds

Chronological data on Wong Ming-Dao

July 1900 Born in Beijing.

1914 Reborn and being saved.

1920 Received God's calling and decided on a life-long ministry.

1921 Forced to leave the school due to his insistence on the truth of baptism and then baptised at Paoting, Hopei.

1921–1924 Mostly devoted to Bible reading, prayers and work at home. Served in Beijing and its vicinity, and began a little gathering at home.

1924 Began his writing ministry at home.

1925 The door of free preaching began to be widely opened, including serving in Beijing and travelling in many provinces of the country to preach.

1925–1926 Preaching in Kiangsu and Chekiang.

1927 Went to the North-east to preach and began to publish *Spiritual Food Quarterly*.

1928 Married at Hangchow and preached in Hopei, Shenyang and other regions in the North-east. Beginning in 1928, he selected his more important essays and published them in book form. From 1928–1948 fifty titles of his books were published.

1929 Preaching in Hopei, Liaoning, Kirin, Anhwei and Shantung.

1930 Preaching in Kiangsu, Anhwei, Kirin, Heilungkiang, Shansi, Suiyuan, Liaoning and Harbin.

1931 Preaching in Kirin, Liaoning, Shantung, Heilungkiang, Anhwei and Chekiang.

1932 Preaching in Shantung, Kiangsu, Hunan, Honan, Kwangtung, Kiangsi and Chekiang.

1933 Preaching in Shantung, Kiangsu, Honan, Anhwei, Hopei, Liaoning and Kirin.

1934 Preaching in Kiangsu, Shantung, Hopei, Shansi, Kwangtung and Kwangsi.

1935 Preaching in Shansi, Shantung, Anhwei, Honan, Shensi, Hopei, Liaoning, Kiangsi and Hupei.

1936 Preaching in Suiyuan, Hopei, Honan, Kwangtung, Kiangsi, Shansi. *The Christian Hymns* published.

1937	Preaching in Kiangsu, Shantung, Kansu and Shensi.
1937	Completion of the Christian Tabernacle.
1938	Preaching in Hopei, Shantung and Suiyuan.
1939	Preaching in Suiyuan, Shansi, Hopei, Shantung, Harbin, Kiangsu and Hong Kong.
1940	Preaching in Shantung, Anhwei, Kirin, Heilungkiang and Jehol.
1941	Preaching in Hopei, Shantung and Honan.
1942	Preaching in Hopei, Honan and Shantung.
1943	Preaching in Hopei, Shantung and Kiangsu.
1944	Preaching in Hopei and Shantung.
1945	Preaching in Hopei.
1946	Preaching in Szechwan, Yunnan, Kweichow and Kiangsu.
1947	Preaching in Hopei. His mother died.
1948	Preaching in Hopei, Shensi, Kiangsu and Anhwei.
1949–1955	Serving in the Christian Tabernacle in Beijing.
1954–1955	Writing four essays in defence of the Christian faith.
1955–1980	Imprisoned.

Sources

The number in brackets at the bottom of each reading indicates the booklet or book, as listed below, from which a message is taken.

Let your light shine before men, that they may see your good deeds and praise your Father in heaven.

Matthew 5:16

There are many different aspects of the Christian life. That which most strongly influences other people and most closely concerns the glory of God, is the Christian's conduct. The reason we must watch and pray, spend time in studying the Bible, regularly meet together and seek biblical truth, is that through these things we may become holier, bring greater glory to God and be better able to help and serve other people.

If we are to bear witness to the Lord, if we are to lead people to the Lord and if we are to unfold the truth to guide people, then we must be given to doing good deeds. For only then can we persuade people to accept what we preach and proclaim.

God looks on our hearts; men look on our deeds. We cannot take our inner faith and love and display them for people to observe. All that we can show to other people are our deeds. Naturally, if we do not first have inner faith and love, we shall never be capable of producing genuine good deeds. But without good deeds, we shall not only fail to express our inner faith, love, sincerity and zeal, but also the question will arise as to whether we do, in fact, possess these qualities. (16)

**Do not be foolish, but understand what the Lord's will
is.**   **Ephesians 5:17**

There is a close relationship between understanding God's
will and being familiar with the Bible. Since the will of God is
revealed in the Scriptures, it naturally follows that the more
familiar we are with the Scriptures, the easier it is to understand God's will.

In order to achieve this familiarity, it is essential that we
spend time in diligent study of the Scriptures, memorising
important passages and turning them over in our minds.

When I read the Bible, it ought to be like a child reading a
letter from his father in a distant place. A child in that
situation would take note of the instructions that his father
gives him – about how he should behave: how he should
honour his parents, conduct himself in the world, love his
brothers and sisters, labour diligently, manage the home and
ward off the seductions of evil men – so that the father,
though separated from the son or daughter, would be happy
and at ease. This would be doing one's duty as a child.

At the same time, the letter would convey to the child his
father's love for him and would announce to him all the
enjoyable benefits that the father is conferring on him.

As a Christian reads the Bible with such an attitude, he
can discern the will of God, and gain maximum benefit from
reading the Scriptures. Those who read the Bible as no more
than a textbook will fail to obtain these blessings. (16)

Month 1: Day 3   A good testimony

**The administrators and the satraps tried to find grounds
for charges against Daniel in his conduct of government
affairs, but they were unable to do so. They could find
no corruption in him, because he was trustworthy and
neither corrupt nor negligent.**   **Daniel 6:4**

This is a splendid testimony to the work of Daniel. The most
outstanding reason for his success was naturally the power
and wisdom that were granted to him as a result of his habit
of praying three times every day. Suppose he had been
careless and indolent – would it have been possible for him to
accomplish what he did?

The fact is, we ought, on the one hand, to ask God to give
us strength and wisdom and, on the other hand, to be diligent
and faithful, watchful and trembling (lest we fail), and to
carry out satisfactorily what is our duty. It is true that God
wants us to put our trust in him and keep our eyes on him; he
also wants us to be diligent and faithful in our work. Only
when there is a blend of these two elements can there be a
good testimony resulting from our work.

The disciples of the Lord ought to be the most industrious,
the most loyal and the most satisfactory workers in the world.
Irrespective of who they are in business for, they should carry
out their tasks as for the Lord. Not only should they cherish
an attitude of faithfulness in doing all that lies before them,
they should also serve in a spirit of love. They should do what
they have to do exuberantly, joyfully and with great expect-
ancy – not in the hope that after doing well they will receive
the praise and recompense of men; but in the hope that when
they meet the Lord they will receive commendation from
him. (16)

**Whether you eat or drink or whatever you do, do it all
for the glory of God. Do not cause anyone to stumble,
whether Jews, Greeks or the church of God – even as I
try to please everybody in every way. For I am not
seeking my own good but the good of many, so that they
may be saved.** **1 Corinthians 10:31–33**

How straightforward are the two principles in these verses!
The first principle is this: Glorify God; and the second: Seek
the good of other people.

The world presents us with innumerable affairs, undertakings and operations, but these two principles are a clear
guide as to what, as Christians, we may or may not do.
Within the scope of these two principles we have freedom
unlimited: there are no words we cannot say; there is nothing
we may not do; there is no object we may not make use of; and
there is no place to which we may not go.

Whatever in the Bible is forbidden, we resolutely avoid.
Whatever in the Bible we are instructed to do, we seek to
carry out word for word. But what of matters that are *not*
mentioned in the Bible? Whatever glorifies God and brings
benefit to other people, we can undertake boldly. Whatever
brings shame to God and causes harm to other people, even
though the Bible has not expressly forbidden it, we shall have
nothing whatever to do with. (16)

[Jesus said:] 'Whoever has my commands and obeys them, he is the one who loves me. He who loves me will be loved by my Father, and I too will love him and show myself to him.' Then Judas (not Judas Iscariot) said, 'But, Lord, why do you intend to show yourself to us and not to the world?' Jesus replied, 'If anyone loves me, he will obey my teaching. My Father will love him, and we will come to him and make our home with him.'

John 14:21–23

Our Lord knows those who truly love him. Even more is he aware of the kind of life lived by those who love him. His words are sufficient to enable us to distinguish between those who truly love him and those who do not truly love him.

If you wish to know whether you do or do not truly love the Lord, you only need to review your thoughts, your ideas, your words, your conduct, your activities and your whole manner of life, checking whether they harmonise with the Lord's commands or not.

Are you sincere and upright, frank and straightforward, in accordance with the Lord's commands? Are you sober and holy, uncontaminated by uncleanness? Are you among those who are kind and compassionate and care for other people? Are you incorruptible and just and entirely free from covetousness? Are you rich in forbearance and do you forgive your enemies? Are you courageous and strong and free from cowardice? Do you hate sin and abhor evil? Do you refrain from indulging yourself in any way?

If you find that you have truly kept the Lord's commands, then you may rest assured that you are one who loves the Lord. But if you find that your manner of life does not harmonise with the Lord's commands, and you even reach the point of entertaining apostasy, then do not deceive yourself or other people any more. (16)

**Whoever has my commands and obeys them, he is the
one who loves me. He who loves me will be loved by my
Father, and I too will love him and show myself to
him . . . If anyone loves me, he will obey my teaching.
My Father will love him, and we will come to him and
make our home with him.   John 14:21–23**

How precious – and how wonderful – are these two promises!
The Father and the Lord will manifest themselves to those
who love him, and will also dwell with them. Can any
privilege in the whole world be greater than this? Can any
happiness be greater than this?

There are many people who declare that they want to love
the Lord, and yet it is to be feared that in the depths of their
hearts they are really afraid to be numbered among those
who love the Lord. For if they truly loved the Lord it would
inevitably involve many inconveniences for the flesh, and
they would suffer considerable losses. They could no longer
tell untruths, or be boastful, or set their minds on becoming
wealthy or famous, or live lives of self-indulgence, or be
covetous, or seek their own interests, or inflict loss on other
people.

What they may fail to realise, however, is that if they truly
love the Lord and obey his commands, even though the flesh
suffers some inconvenience and they encounter losses, it will
not be long before they experience a life that is abundant in
joy and glory, and precious beyond measure.

The most important things that anyone can do are to put
their trust in the Lord and inherit his salvation and to love
the Lord and inherit his promises. (16)

As for you, son of man, your countrymen are talking
together about you by the walls and at the doors of the
houses, saying to each other, 'Come and hear the message that has come from the Lord.' My people come to
you, as they usually do, and sit before you to listen to
your words, but they do not put them into practice. With
their mouths they express devotion, but their hearts are
greedy for unjust gain. Indeed, to them you are nothing
more than one who sings love songs with a beautiful
voice and plays an instrument well, for they hear your
words but do not put them into practice.

                                        Ezekiel 33:30–32

We see here how assiduously the Israelites met together. We
see how happy they were to listen to the prophets when they
preached the word of God. All the people made a point of
sitting before the prophets and listening to their teaching.
They appeared to be devout people of God. However, we
read that they 'listen to your words, but they do not put them
into practice.' We read also that 'their hearts are greedy for
unjust gain.' These people had not yet acknowledged God in
their hearts but they were happy to listen to this preaching.
Why was this so?

The reason they sought to hear God's words was obviously
not that they desired to act in accordance with them. Rather,
it was because they regarded the prophet as 'one who sings
love songs with a beautiful voice and plays an instrument
well.' They listened to the preaching not in order to profit
spiritually; still less to enhance their manner of life. They
came together to listen to the preaching because Ezekiel's
illustrations were apt and his choice of words was felicitous;
he spoke fluently and his sympathy moved people. Afterwards those who had listened purely to please their ears and
not to enhance their manner of life would not experience any
change or progress in the way they lived. (16)

Israel has sinned; they have violated my covenant, which I commanded them to keep. They have taken some of the devoted things; they have stolen, they have lied, they have put them with their own possessions. That is why the Israelites cannot stand against their enemies; they turn their backs and run because they have been made liable to destruction. I will not be with you any more unless you destroy whatever among you is devoted to destruction.   **Joshua 7:11, 12**

Why is the present-day church a defeated church? Why is the condition of believers so pitiful? Why do those engaged in sacred work lose their power? It is because there are things among them that ought to be destroyed. Otherwise, the Lord would long ago have done great things among us.

The Lord's words will never come to nothing. We do not need to enquire into other matters; all we need to do is to ask ourselves whether we are hindering the fulfilment of God's promises.

What kind of thing is it that hinders what God wants to do? It is secret sin. That which most harms an individual believer or a church is not open but hidden sin.

My friends! The hidden things under the tent that ought to be destroyed are the sins of the heart, such as avarice, worship of mammon, craftiness, treachery, sham, hatred, envy, licentiousness, impurity, pride and arrogance, and the sin of loving the world more than loving God. These are the buried things that ought to be done away with. These are the things that cause us to be defeated in the face of the enemy. They are the things that hinder the church from revival and bring defeat to those engaged in sacred work. (4)

I will show you what he is like who comes to me and hears my words and puts them into practice.   Luke 6:47

My food . . . is to do the will of him who sent me and to finish his work.   John 4:34

In these verses the Lord makes reference to two related matters: putting his words into practice, and finishing his work. Our Lord was able to finish the Father's work *only* because he did the Father's will.

There are many zealous believers today who only emphasise the doing of God's *work* and fail to emphasise the doing of God's *will*. Since they have overlooked this basic requirement they are not able, in the work of God, to ensure any worthwhile achievement.

There are many zealous preachers today who engage in the work only for a limited period, and then lose their power and testimony, becoming a stumbling-block to others, because they only stress the work and lightly regard the matter of living a devout life.

There is a vast difference between doing the work of God and doing the work of the world. People who possess ability and resolution, even though they lack an upright character, can be brilliantly successful in literature, in the arts, in architecture, in industry, in military matters and in politics. But it is impossible for those who lack an upright character to achieve true success in the work of God. (16)

**Why do you call me, 'Lord, Lord,' and do not do what I
say?**   **Luke 6:46**

The themes chosen by many so-called spiritually-minded
preachers when preaching to believers admittedly all consist
of biblical truth, yet only a limited amount of their preaching
is concerned with the practical aspects of Christian living.
They regard teaching about the practical issues of life as
being too superficial, and they prefer to preach doctrines that
are profound and abstruse.

The fact is, they cannot and they dare not preach on these
practical matters. Those who themselves have not personally
experienced a particular facet of teaching are in no position
to preach it to others. Also, those whose manner of life is not
what it ought to be, are reluctant to preach on these doctrines. Since their way of life is on a plane no higher than that
of many others, they avoid preaching on these practical
matters. By concentrating on certain profound doctrines,
they escape the reproof of their own consciences and the
rebuke of other people at the same time.

The audience for its part is also happier to listen to
'spiritual' doctrines, for this emphasis seals off and keeps out
of sight the sins in their lives.

For these reasons, it may be only rarely that we hear
preachers who deal with the practical issues in our lives. (16)

I urge you, brothers, in view of God's mercy, to offer your bodies as living sacrifices, holy and pleasing to God – which is your spiritual worship.   Romans 12:1, 2

It is the will of God that all his children should present themselves to him. God then puts them in different places, environments and occupations – in accordance with his perfect will – where they may serve him. Although the occupations of these believers differ, if all are diligent and faithful in their respective spheres and occupations, and if they serve God well and glorify him, then they are all doing God's work. All are serving God; all are pleasing him; and all will receive his reward.

We must on no account regard the Christian who is engaged in preaching as possessing a higher status, or as being more spiritual than believers engaged in other types of work, or think of all occupations other than preaching as being fleshly and worldly. Even though a Christian is engaged in 'secular' work, so long as he cherishes an attitude of serving God, he is no less pleasing to God than the one whose occupation is preaching. Indeed, if a preacher is not faithful and does not love God and is only preaching for a living or for vainglory, he is vastly inferior in the sight of God to a Christian who is faithfully serving God in another occupation. (16)

Depart, depart, go out from there! Touch no unclean thing! Come out from it and be pure, you who carry the vessels of the Lord.   **Isaiah 52:11**

To be engaged in carrying the vessels of God is to be serving God; to be engaged in sacred ministry for God. God is holy. The vessels of God are holy. So those who carry the vessels of God should be holy too. Those who are unclean can by no means participate in this sacred ministry.

Why is it that those who today engage in sacred ministry, though many times more numerous than those who did so in times of old, fall far short in their achievements? The most outstanding reason is that some of those who participate in sacred ministry are not pure.

I have observed many so-called believers who do not differ greatly from unbelievers. True, they may read the Bible and pray; attend a place of worship; sing hymns and listen to the preaching of the word; contribute to God's treasury. But otherwise their lives differ little from those of unbelievers. Is any difference to be observed in their words, their conduct, their ideas and purposes? If there is no marked difference in these things, we ought not to be surprised at their failures. For those whom God chooses and uses are the sanctified ones.

Are you yourself conscious that God wants to appoint you to participate in sacred ministry? If you are, I urge you to purify yourself. When you purify yourself, you will receive power from above. And God will greatly use you. (4)

'Why have we fasted,' they say, 'and you have not seen it? Why have we humbled ourselves and you have not noticed?' Yet on the day of your fasting, you do as you please and exploit all your workers.   **Isaiah 58:3**

The reason that the devotion of the people of Israel failed to please God, although they described themselves with their own lips as devout, was that in their deeds they rebelled against God's commands. They spoke of loving the God of heaven but for the people around them they had not the slightest love whatever. With their lips they uttered sentiments of love but in their hearts they still pursued wealth and gain.

Look at the way in which they profited themselves! 'On the day of your fasting, you do as you please and exploit all your workers.' Those who hope to be the recipients of God's compassion but are unwilling to have compassion on other people, can in no way be blessed by God. God is a God of love but those who are concerned only to profit themselves are in opposition to him. A life of self-pleasing is one that God hates.

How can a person who is in opposition to God, and who practises the things that God hates, expect to be acceptable to God and blessed by him? If a believer has only eyes for himself, for wealth, for fame, for pleasure and for gain, if he exerts all his strength to amass possessions for himself and shows no concern about the needs and troubles of other people, then, no matter how pious his words may sound and no matter what other external appearances there are, God can in no way acknowledge him as one who is truly devout. (2)

The price and rewards of pleasing God

We speak as men approved by God to be entrusted with the gospel. We are not trying to please men but God, who tests our hearts.   **1 Thessalonians 2:4**

There are some believers who understand that they ought to be single-hearted in their efforts to please God but, because they take other matters into consideration, they dare not be so. Some fear that they will suffer loss; some fear that they will suffer persecution. Since we are still in the body, it is quite natural and not in any way strange that we should fear to suffer loss or shame or persecution. But what God looks for is that for his sake we should be willing to suffer all these things.

Our willingness to suffer loss, shame and persecution shows that we fear and worship, honour and love God. Because of this, he will certainly bestow his blessings on us. The loss that we suffer in order to please God, will in the end be converted into profit; the shame that we suffer in order to please God, will in the end be converted into glory; and the persecution that we suffer in order to please God, will in the end be converted into blessing.

In order to please God, Abraham was once willing to offer up his son Isaac, who had been born in his old age. When God saw his aim and his obedience, he did not permit him to put Isaac to death; on the contrary, God bestowed abundant blessing on him. (16)

Woe to you, teachers of the law and Pharisees, you hypocrites!   Matthew 23:23

Hypocrisy is a very grave sin (Matthew 23:23–28). It is also a sin that believers fall into very easily. No matter how fine a Christian is, if he stresses only external things and neglects inner things, it can lead to his falling into the sin of hypocrisy.

The only way to prevent hypocrisy entering into our lives is to allow Christ to dwell in our hearts all the time: to recognise him as both Lord and King; to allow him to use his authority to drive out all evil and unrighteousness and guard our hearts and thoughts, words and deeds. In that way, our whole lives will be lived in his light and we shall be worthy disciples.

Let us come in all sincerity into the presence of the Lord and allow his light to shine on us so that we can perceive our own shortcomings and failures. If we find that we have already fallen into the sin of hypocrisy, we should repent without delay; we should confess this terrible sin and put it away. If we have not yet fallen into this sin, we should be vigilant and watchful and look to God to keep us so that we on no account fall in this way. (16)

Let those who love the Lord hate evil.   **Psalm 97:10**

It is the duty of Christians to learn how to love; to learn how to be compassionate; to learn how to be tolerant; to learn how to forgive; to learn how to sympathise; and to learn how to endure.

At the same time, they must learn how to hate. It is not, of course, *people* whom they must learn to hate; it is *evil*. The things that God himself hates include the following: the concourse of evil men; the deeds of those who rebel against him; all false ways; lying; those who hate God and attack him. Therefore those who worship God also hate these things. Those who witness these evil actions and observe these evil men and remain completely untroubled by them are, in God's sight, assuredly lacking in devotion. They are certainly not 100 per cent like God; nor do they love God 100 per cent. No matter how impressive are the virtues of a believer, if he still does not hate evil, that is a serious deficiency and a very grave weakness.

The world today is choked with wickedness; the church is laced with apostasy. Yet many zealous believers can still see and hear these things without any feeling of sorrow or revulsion. Indeed, they often regard these things as of no consequence. This is enough to demonstrate that even among zealous believers there are comparatively few who are really of one mind with God and who truly love him. (16)

Is not this the kind of fasting I have chosen . . . ? Is it not to share your food with the hungry and to provide the poor wanderer with shelter – when you see the naked, to clothe him, and not to turn away from your own flesh and blood?   **Isaiah 58:6, 7**

Blessed are the merciful, for they will be shown mercy.   **Matthew 5:7**

It is not until a believer shows concern and compassion for those in trouble around him that he demonstrates the reality of his love for God.

I suggest that you investigate how many people around you are suffering in either body or spirit and how urgently they need the compassion and help of other people. You ought to do all that you can, in a judicious way, to help and relieve them.

The greatest commandment in the Law is, 'Love the Lord your God with all your heart and with all your soul and with all your mind and with all your strength,' and the second is, 'Love your neighbour as yourself' (Mark 12:29–31). If you obey God's commands, you will be pleasing him and enjoying the blessings he bestows.

Many people think of piety as referring only to prayer, worship, singing, presenting our offerings, reading the Bible and preaching the word. It is often overlooked that true devotion cannot be separated from a believer's everyday life. God is certainly pleased that we engage in disciplines such as prayer. But even more does he want us, through these, to learn how to get rid of the things that he abhors – such as self-seeking and inflicting suffering on other people – and to do the things that are pleasing to him – such as loving one's neighbour as oneself. (2)

Month 1: Day 18   Loving others

Jesus replied: 'Love the Lord your God with all your heart and with all your soul and with all your mind. This is the first and greatest commandment. And the second is like it: "Love your neighbour as yourself."'

Matthew 22:37–39

You should regard the practice of worshipping God as the foundation on which you establish yourself in life; and you should regard love of your neighbour as the basis of your relationships in the world.

In all your dealings with other people be absolutely sincere. When you experience poverty, do not flatter people; in times of affluence do not be proud.

Do not harbour envy in your heart. When other people enjoy benefits, rejoice with them. Don't take pleasure in other people's misfortunes. When you encounter people in trouble, make a point of sharing their grief. When you are sharing accommodation with other people and opportunities to secure benefits present themselves, do not force your way in front. But when danger looms ahead, do not shelter behind other people and hold back. If you have inadvertently taken advantage of other people, then acknowledge your fault and make reparation. If you have been taken advantage of by other people, then be tolerant and forgiving.

Whenever property passes through your hands, irrespective of whether it is much or little, you must be extremely careful and scrupulously honest. In all your associations with friends, whether male or female, be upright and pure in mind. Do not lightly make promises but when you do make promises, do everything possible to carry them out. Do not lightly borrow from people but when you do borrow anything, then strive to repay it as soon as possible.

Respect your elders; respect other people's elders. Love your own children and love other people's children. (5)

The Lord detests lying lips, but he delights in men who are truthful.   **Proverbs 12:22**

Without any question the world is full of deceitfulness and lying. But Christians ought to be 'blameless and pure, children of God without fault in a crooked and depraved generation' (Philippians 2:15).

However, when Christians do live up to these standards, they inevitably encounter persecution from the world. The more a Christian is like his Lord, the more he will be persecuted by the world.

Why are the disciples of Christ subject to this persecution by the world? It is not merely because they confess the Lord's name; it is even more because they have put the Lord's words into practice. No matter what price we have to pay and what sacrifice we have to make, we must never fear to confess the name of the Lord. And no matter what price we have to pay or what sacrifice we have to make, we must never fear to put the Lord's words into practice.

So we ought to be prepared to be people of sincerity and truth. If, because we are unwilling to utter untruths, we are reviled and attacked or if, because we are unwilling to follow others along the path of hypocrisy, we encounter trouble and persecution – then we are blessed indeed. For this is to suffer persecution for righteousness. 'Blessed are those who are persecuted because of righteousness, for theirs is the kingdom of heaven' (Matthew 5:10). (17)

Peter asked her, 'Tell me, is this the price you and
Ananias got for the land?' 'Yes,' she said, 'that is the
price.'   Acts 5:8

Many believers today are like those described in Acts 5:1–11
in that they utter untruths in order to achieve fame. Although
their love is not very deep, they want other people to say that
it is. The work in which they are engaged is not particularly
good but they want people to say that it is. Their life is not
particularly pious but they want people to say that it is. They
have not laboured on behalf of other people to the point of
becoming fatigued but they want other people to say that
they have. They have not made any striking sacrifices for the
Lord but they want people to say that they have. They thus
resort to telling lies as the only way to attain their objective of
becoming persons of repute.

   Their lying takes various forms. It may simply be a case of
exaggeration; it may be making something out of nothing,
the fabrication of facts; or it may simply be a case of robbing
other people of their rightful merit by claiming it for oneself.
The practice of giving utterance to untruths in order to gain
prestige is not at all uncommon in the churches today. It is
particularly grievous that many church leaders set this kind
of example and thus encourage ordinary believers to do the
same. (17)

Month 1: Day 21   No stealing

**He who has been stealing must steal no longer, but must
work, doing something useful with his own hands, that
he may have something to share with those in need.**

Ephesians 4:28

Let us consider for a moment the meaning of stealing. If an
official takes articles that are public property and makes
personal use of them in his own home, that is stealing. When
the head of an organisation receives certain gifts from someone and then bestows on that benefactor a position in the
organisation, that is stealing.

When a person helps his relatives or friends to make a train
journey or boat trip without a ticket or facilitates their entry
into an area requiring tickets without their having to buy a
ticket, that is stealing. When a person who works in the
dispensary of a hospital takes medicine against hospital
regulations for his own personal use or for the use of a friend,
that also is stealing.

To take advantage of a person's absence in order to read
his correspondence clandestinely is also stealing.

If we ought to offer something to God but keep it back for
our own use – that is stealing. If by devious methods we deny
glory to God and arrogate it to ourselves, that too is stealing.

These examples are all characterised by the use of im-
proper and dishonourable methods to get hold of things that
do not belong to us and which ought not to be in our hands;
therefore, they all constitute stealing. (17)

He who has been stealing must steal no longer, but must work, doing something useful with his own hands, that he may have something to share with those in need.
Ephesians 4:28

There are believers who are upright and disciplined in regard to their possessions, none of which have been obtained dishonestly, but who tend to be lazy and indolent in their lives. Of these there are not a few. They find it difficult to make themselves work and, as a consequence, they grow more and more incapable of working. They become short of food and clothing, and they thus find it necessary to beg other people for help. They then become a burden to others and cause God to be dishonoured. People of this character ought to rid themselves of the sin of idleness.

There are some zealous believers who use their enthusiasm and their willingness to serve God as a pretext for being lazy and doing nothing. They explain the situation by saying that they want to serve God but that God has not given them any work to do. In actual fact, they are not really worthy to be involved in the work of God, for even in the work of man they have not acquitted themselves well. Since they are incapable of doing the work of God, and since they are unwilling to carry out the duties of ordinary life, what can they be but wastrels, living by sponging off others and profiting by what has been produced through the labours of other people? This is truly a form of stealing. (17)

Keep your lives free from the love of money and be content with what you have, because God has said, 'Never will I leave you; never will I forsake you.'

Hebrews 13:5

We must bear in mind that money is among the commodities that God has entrusted to us. The most appropriate and the safest way of acquiring money is to earn it by our labour. Do not hanker after money that is not produced by your own toil and labour. To cherish such a hope is simply avarice. Do not occasion loss to other people in order that you yourself may enjoy gain, for that is equivalent to stealing.

Do not accept money that you suspect to be a bribe. Do not amass money by gambling or by anything akin to gambling. Do not set out to get money by striving with people. When a Christian strives with people to gain possession of some property, no matter whether he has right on his side or not, he has already failed in the sight of God, while in the sight of men he has lost his testimony.

When you make an acquisition do not forget to take out the proportion that is due to God and offer it up to him.

Make up your mind not to borrow money from other people if it can possibly be avoided. Give generously towards the relief of those in need. Do not lay up for yourselves vast amounts of money. Nor should you hoard vast amounts for your children. Do not spend money extravagantly with a view to acquiring empty glory. Seek in all things to be economical. (5)

**Flee from sexual immorality. All other sins a man
commits are outside his body, but he who sins sexually
sins against his own body.**   **1 Corinthians 6:18**

The apostle Paul made a point of warning believers against
sexual immorality. For 'he who sins sexually sins against his
own body,' and thus defiles the temple of God.

How widespread is the sin of immorality and how easy it is
for believers to sin in this way! The eyes of many believers are
taken up with lust and their hearts are full of impure
thoughts. They read unwholesome publications; they watch
lascivious films; they participate in unsavoury talk. Many
believers fall in love with people of the opposite sex other
than their own partners. The relationship begins with
friendship and it then develops into love. Finally it reaches
the point of sexual immorality.

Yet if we bear in mind that our bodies are the temple of
God and that the Spirit of God dwells within us; if we recall
again that we have been bought by God at the high price of
the blood of the Lord Jesus, his Son, how could we want to
defile our bodies through immoral conduct? (16)

He who conceals his sins does not prosper, but whoever confesses and renounces them finds mercy.

Proverbs 28:13

When a Christian falls into sin, if he sincerely confesses the sin and repents in the presence of God, then God will forgive him. But if he does not confess his sin, not only is the sin not forgiven but also he is likely to commit an even greater sin – by telling an untruth to cover it up. The sin of telling an untruth in order to cover up a sin already committed, is even greater than the original sin in that it is designed to deceive God. The more we resort to untruths in order to cover up sin, the harder our hearts become, and if this is not dealt with, we shall find ourselves in a situation beyond recovery.

We must always be alert, and when we fall into sin we must on no account use untruths to cover this up. No matter whether we are in the presence of men or in the presence of God, we must speak sincerely. It is better to be disparaged by men on account of our sin than to tell untruths and offend God. For even though we are temporarily dishonoured through our sin, we will afterwards be raised up again by God. Not only will God bless us in his presence, he will also enable us to be respected and trusted in the sight of men. But if we aim to escape temporary shame and therefore tell untruths to cover up our sin, we will fall even further into sin and this will eventually call forth great dishonour and anathemas. (17)

Do you not know that your body is a temple of the Holy Spirit, who is in you, whom you have received from God? You are not your own; you were bought at a price. Therefore honour God with your body.

1 Corinthians 6:19, 20

The temple today is not a building set up with men's hands; it consists of the bodies of the saints. The place where believers gather for worship ought to be called a place of worship or an assembly hall. It should certainly not be designated a temple.

What a wonderful truth this is! What a precious reality! For our bodies to be the temple of God is certainly something that would never have occurred to us. We are people who have long been sunk in sin, who have been infected with uncleanness and unrighteousness, who have given rein to shameful lusts and who have, in every way, become enemies of God. Yet in spite of our having been people like this, we are cleansed through the blood of Christ and anointed by the Holy Spirit and we become the temple where God abides. When people who have been corrupted like ourselves are forgiven and accepted by God, we feel that we have already been treated with grace beyond all expectation. Who would have thought that God would be willing to take our bodies as the temple in which he can live?

The temple of God! How great, how sacred, how exalted is this designation! The Spirit of God abides in this temple. He wants this temple to manifest his glory and to display his compassion. It is his purpose that the temple should be the means of great blessing to many people. When we know of a certainty what God wants to do through our bodies, how joyful and how grateful we should be! At the same time how vigilant and how watchful we should be. (16)

Let love and faithfulness never leave you; bind them around your neck, write them on the tablet of your heart. Then you will win favour and a good name in the sight of God and man.   **Proverbs 3:3, 4**

Selfishness is the source of all sin. And deceit is the screen that covers sins of all kinds.

All kinds of evil arise because of selfishness – hatred, covetousness, immorality, envy, pride, assault, murder, stealing, plundering and so on. And then, in order to cover it up, offenders add lying and deceit. If we do not get rid of the two sins of self-seeking and deceit, then all the sins that arise because of them will multiply and spread further. As a consequence those concerned will go from bad to worse until they are embroiled in some calamity.

On the other hand, if we make sure that these two precious things – love and faithfulness – never leave us, we shall drive away the two frightening sins of selfishness and deceit. Once we rid ourselves of selfishness and deceit, all the other sins will lose their support and be denied the screens that cover them. The people who have love and compassion will not be found harming other people, and those who are faithful and sincere will not act falsely; nor will they think up untruths to cover their own faults.

Therefore, those who carry with them these two valuables, and bind them around their necks, will not only be delivered from the attacks of selfishness and deceit but will also, at the same time, drive out other sins – great and small. For love and compassion, with sincerity and faithfulness, can not only bring us happiness, they can also be a safeguard against disaster. How extensive is the sphere of their usefulness! (17)

Let love and faithfulness never leave you; bind them around your neck, write them on the tablet of your heart. Then you will win favour and a good name in the sight of God and man.   **Proverbs 3:3, 4**

God not only enjoins us to wear these two precious things – love and faithfulness – he also tells us of the advantages and favours that they obtain for us: 'Then you will win favour and a good name in the sight of God and man.'

God is a loving God and a faithful God. So all those who possess the two virtues of love and faithfulness, are in these respects like God. They will be pleasing to God and they will win his favour. In the sight of God they are wise.

At the same time, those who possess these two virtues will win respect in the sight of men; they will win men's trust; and in the sight of men they will be wise. If a person invariably treats other people with love and compassion and considers other people and strives to make them happy, he will, without question, win people's love and respect. If a person is invariably sincere and without artificiality, if he is inwardly and outwardly consistent, if he neither tells untruths nor engages in deceit, if he is loyal in his friendships, if he shows sincerity in his relations with others and if he always keeps his promises – could such a person do other than win people's trust? (17)

I am the good shepherd. The good shepherd lays down his life for the sheep. The hired hand is not the shepherd who owns the sheep. So when he sees the wolf coming, he abandons the sheep and runs away. Then the wolf attacks the flock and scatters it. The man runs away because he is a hired hand and cares nothing for the sheep.   **John 10:11–13**

Among all the people who bear responsibility for the leadership of churches throughout the world, there are many who can only be described as hired labourers. They undertake the ministry of pastoring not as a result of loving the Lord and loving the Lord's flock but because they depend on this for their livelihood.

When you get down to it, you find that people of this nature have no concern in their heart for the flock of God. Their concern is not about dangers to the flock or the safety of the flock; their concern is to protect their own interests. At a time of calm and stability, they work in the church (diligently, perhaps) and receive a salary. Yet if one day the path ahead should be threatened with danger, they would soon turn their backs on the sheep and flee elsewhere.

Pastors of this nature, who may be compared to hirelings, are all too numerous. So the church is desolate and the church is scattered.

Serving as good shepherds of the flock is no easy task. For such shepherds must be men of unimpeachable virtue and abundant love. They also need to prepare constantly to suffer loss, to meet adversity and to face persecution, for the Lord and for his flock. But to do this is not really their loss; it is their happiness. For when the great Shepherd – the Lord Jesus Christ – is manifested, they will receive a crown of glory. (14)

It was just before the Passover Feast. Jesus knew that the time had come for him to leave this world and go to the Father. Having loved his own who were in the world, he now showed them the full extent of his love.   John 13:1

Why does the Lord love us? It is not because we have any good points; nor is it because we have any lovable features. In the sight of the Lord we are like one whose body is full of sores. He loves us when we are good; and when we are bad he loves us no less. He loves us when we are strong and victorious; and when we are weak and defeated he loves us no less. He loves us when we are lovable; and he loves us no less when we are unlovable. It is not because of what we are that he loves us; it is because his love is a wonderful love.

Once we have got a grasp of this truth, we need not again be downcast or despairing on account of our failures. Even less, when we have stumbled and fallen into sin, should we imagine that the Lord has cast us off. After stumbling, we should immediately get up and press ahead. When we fall into sin, we should repent and confess our sin before the Lord immediately. We should trust again in the Lord's grace and strength to enable us to battle with the devil.

Since the Lord loves us in this way, we ought not to misunderstand him again. Nor should we adopt human attitudes as a standard by which to measure the attitudes of the Lord and as a consequence become ungrateful for his great and wonderful love. (19)

Do not be afraid of what you are about to suffer. I tell you, the devil will put some of you in prison to test you, and you will suffer persecution for ten days. Be faithful, even to the point of death, and I will give you the crown of life.   **Revelation 2:10**

If we have an opportunity to lay down our lives for the Lord, that is truly an experience that cannot be bettered. But what if we have no opportunity to do this? Are we not very unfortunate?

This question is easily answered. Although comparatively few believers have the opportunity to lay down their lives for the Lord, every believer can still be a victorious warrior of this kind. All that is needed is that we possess similar faith, courage and determination; that we are *prepared* to lay down our lives for the Lord; that in all circumstances we press boldly ahead; that we eschew timidity; that we do not allow ourselves to be carried along by the currents of the world; that we neither dishonour the Lord's name nor disobey his commands; and that we are not insensible of the Lord's commission and expectations.

Even though we may never have the opportunity to lay down our lives for the Lord, we may still obtain the glory and reward which is won by those who actually do so. For what the Lord requires is wholehearted loyalty. If we are wholeheartedly loyal, whether we have the opportunity to lay down our lives for him or not, we shall still be welcomed and honoured by the Lord. (11)

'They will fight against you but will not overcome you, for I am with you and will rescue you,' declares the Lord.   **Jeremiah 1:19**

Endure hardship with us like a good soldier of Christ Jesus.   **2 Timothy 2:3**

The church today is darkened and corrupt. In these respects it has reproduced the characteristics of the world. With an environment like this, it is truly an immensely difficult task to preach the word of God faithfully.

Speaking from the point of view of the flesh, I am quite unwilling to create even a single enemy. It is totally against my inclination to provoke even a single person to inveigh against me or slander me. My desire, on the contrary, is that all people should treat me with affection and respect. What I long for is to be welcomed wherever I go and to win the commendation of my fellow-men.

But what is the actual situation? I find that if I wish to be faithful to God, I must endure the ridicule, invective, insults and castigation of many people. These are truly experiences that my flesh would shrink from. But God does not permit me to pander to my 'face' and reputation. His call and his commission drive me on, while his grace and his power have ever afforded me protection. It is because of this that I have been enabled, without fear and without flinching, to proclaim the message that he wants me to proclaim.

This policy has in fact been the means of my making many friends in the various places to which I have gone. Inevitably it also means that I have made enemies. But I can still give thanks to God, for the promise that he made to Jeremiah has also proved true in my own experience. (10)

Month 2: Day 3   The temptation to compromise

Woe to you when all men speak well of you, for that is how their fathers treated the false prophets.   Luke 6:26

There was one particular period in my ministry when the devil put an unworthy thought in my heart. So far as I recollect, I had already visited most of the provinces of China and more people than I can estimate had become acquainted with me. Among these people were many who looked up to me and respected me.

So the question arose in my heart: Why should I continue to follow the policies which I had followed in the past and which were likely to provoke ridicule, opposition and attack? The thought occurred to me that I could eliminate the expressions that wound people's feelings, I could cease to preach the doctrines that some people regarded as superstition and I could desist from sternly rebuking the things that were sinful and apostate. By restraining myself in this way, I would surely cease to call forth the hostile reactions of those who were antagonistic. In this way, I would not only maintain the respect in which I was already held and preserve my reputation, but also win even greater honour. In addition to that, I would no longer be misunderstood, opposed and attacked. In fact I would surely come to be numbered among the great personalities most highly esteemed in the church.

But – thanks be to God! – as soon as these thoughts arose in my heart I realised that they came from the devil. And I had no intention whatsoever of becoming the captive of the devil. Even less was I prepared to rebel against God. Without any compunction, therefore, I rejected the devil's temptation and set my sights on being faithful to God until the end. (10)

If any man builds on this foundation using gold, silver, costly stones, wood, hay or straw, his work will be shown for what it is, because the Day will bring it to light. It will be revealed with fire, and the fire will test the quality of each man's work.   1 Corinthians 3:12, 13

At no time after leading an evangelistic meeting, have I reckoned up the number of people who professed to believe in the Lord and be saved. Nor have I any machinery for preparing such statistics. For not all of those who give some outward sign of believing in the Lord have genuinely repented and put their trust in the Lord. And those who *have* genuinely repented and believed in the Lord are not necessarily all numbered among those who give some outward sign.

Further, some of those who give an outward sign of believing may have an ulterior motive: they may hope to marry a believer or to gain some social standing through the church.

Yet there are certain preachers who are quite prepared to include people of all these categories in their statistics of those who become believers at their meetings. Announcements are sometimes made such as the following: Evangelistic meetings were held at such-and-such a place and lasted for so many days; this number (so many hundreds, etc.) of people believed and were saved. There are also preachers who use all kinds of artificial methods in order to bring pressure on people to give some outward sign of repenting and believing in the Lord, and those who do might be included in the statistics of those saved at the meeting.

Every time I encounter such a situation, I become grieved for those concerned. I have frequently drawn attention to these mistaken policies both in my speaking and in my writing. For the Bible plainly warns preachers not to use wood, hay or straw in their building work.

Guard yourselves and all the flock of which the Holy Spirit has made you overseers. Be shepherds of the church of God, which he bought with his own blood.

Acts 20:28

In order to become an overseer of the whole flock, it is most important that a person should be appointed by the Holy Spirit. In this way he will be equipped to shepherd the whole flock.

Bearing all this in mind, we realise what a great weight of responsibility is borne by overseers. Theirs is a commission of the utmost importance. It is the more necessary, therefore, that they watch for themselves and that they watch for the flock. It is plain that if those who shepherd the flock are ordained only at the hands of men and not by the Holy Spirit, then they are not qualified in essentials to be overseers of the flock.

Suppose we were to undertake an investigation today to find out the nature of leaders in the churches – their beliefs, the manner of their lives, their aims, their characters, their virtues and their work. I am afraid that we should have to come to the conclusion that many of them have never been appointed by the Holy Spirit. There are, of course, many causes of the corruption that now characterises so much of the life of the church, but it has to be said that one of the foremost of these is the fact that many leaders are not appointed by the Holy Spirit. The church of the present day needs to undergo a fundamental change, but unless more believers are appointed by the Holy Spirit to be overseers of the flock, it will be difficult indeed to visualise true revival. (10)

As a prisoner for the Lord . . . I urge you to live a life worthy of the calling you have received.   Ephesians 4:1

In every local church you will find believers who well understand the basic truths of the Bible and yet whose manner of life is marred by many shortcomings. You will find pride, love of fame, vanity, untruthfulness, covetousness, unchastity, envy, slander, hatred, defamation, failure to keep agreements, malpractices, selfishness, party spirit, divisiveness, disloyalty and other forms of sin.

It is in the light of this that I invariably place great emphasis on the believer's manner of life. I repeatedly remind the people of God to glorify him in their lives and, through a holy life and noble character, to testify to the grace of the Lord Jesus Christ. This means to live 'a life worthy of the calling you have received.'

A person who lacks a good character is basically unfit to be engaged in the work of God. If those who serve God do not help believers to develop Christlike characters, their work can never be strong or satisfactory. The teaching of the Lord Jesus Christ consistently stresses the importance of upright living. The letters of the apostles, too, invariably instruct the churches to follow this path.

Is this a matter that those who serve God today can afford to neglect? (10)

Am I now trying to win the approval of men, or of God? Or am I trying to please men? If I were still trying to please men, I would not be a servant of Christ.

Galatians 1:10

Those who have the responsibility of leadership in the churches must distinguish clearly between truth and error, and between right and wrong. In this matter, moreover, they must be absolutely unyielding and uncompromising. Whatever is in harmony with the truth must be carried out positively; and all that is contrary to the truth must be strictly rejected.

In order to carry out such a policy, we must be free from fear. We cannot afford to be afraid of things like misunderstanding, opposition and persecution. Yet church leaders are in danger of being swayed by considerations of 'face.' Whenever church leaders fear to give offence, whenever they fear misunderstanding and opposition, whenever they fear to encounter persecution or danger and whenever, because of these fears, they compromise with policies that do not harmonise with the Scriptures and yield or submit to apostasy, they will certainly lose power and authority. The church will also deteriorate and become corrupt.

If you desire to be a faithful servant of God you must resist the pursuit of wealth and fame; you must also be unsparing of your very life. If you choose otherwise, you will undoubtedly be timid and weak and give way to excessive fear; you will compromise with Satan and you will yield to sin.

Church leaders are like commanders in the army. When an army is about to go into battle, if the commanders are hesitant, cringing or fearful, the whole army will be radically affected. In that event there will be no victory and no song of triumph for hesitant, cringing or fearful commanders and their troops. (10)

The overseer must be above reproach, the husband of but one wife, temperate, self-controlled, respectable, hospitable, able to teach, not given to much wine, not violent but gentle, not quarrelsome, not a lover of money.   **1 Timothy 3:2, 3**

Whenever we are called upon to set apart believers to undertake ministerial responsibility, we must emphasise first of all their beliefs and their character (see 1 Timothy 3:2–13). As for gifts and ability, knowledge and education, they must all be regarded as secondary. When it comes to money and possessions, these are items to which basically we give no consideration at all.

I have often been an observer of churches in the process of setting aside believers to undertake ministerial responsibility, and I have found that what many of these churches emphasise in a leader are his possessions and his money. So long as a believer has money, they will respect him and elevate him; they will ask him to take responsibility and choose him as leader. Their main hope is that he will help the church financially. But as soon as a church begins to follow such a path, it will inevitably degenerate and become corrupt. A policy such as this may be compared to Israel's worship of the golden calf.

The fact is, when someone who has previously been well-to-do and highly placed in society believes in the Lord, it is not good that he should immediately be given responsibility in the church. As a consequence of being wealthy and highly placed in society, he may have been accorded widespread esteem and respect and this may have engendered a spirit of pride and self-importance. People like this need, therefore, to be specially dealt with by the Lord. For if the adulation of believers is added to that of society, they may become even prouder. (10)

**No one can serve two masters. Either he will hate the
one and love the other, or he will be devoted to the one
and despise the other. You cannot serve both God and
money.**   Matthew 6:24

The primary concern of many people who do not believe in
God is to make money. The reason is that since they do not
believe in almighty God, there is nothing in their world that
is more powerful than money.

Alas! The church of the present day appears to be taking
the same path as that of unbelievers. It is to money and not to
God that they give the pre-eminence. Many churches when
preparing to undertake some project, do not first kneel down
and pray to seek God's guidance and help. Their main
concern is to consider ways and means of raising funds. The
most important person in the church is not the spiritual
leader but rather the chairman of the appeals committee.

And what about the posters affixed to the pillars in the
church building? What will you find? Will you find texts,
such as: Commit your way to the Lord; trust in him and he
will do this? I'm afraid not. You will be more likely to find
words such as: What's the use of simply talking about
trusting God? To achieve anything you still need ample
funds. That is how erroneous concepts (such as, 'Money is
almighty'), embraced by those who do not believe in God,
become deeply entrenched also in the minds of many Christians. In effect many churches drive God away and erect a
gigantic altar to mammon. (19)

'Be careful,' Jesus said to them. 'Be on your guard against the yeast of the Pharisees and Sadducees.'
Matthew 16:6

The church's greatest danger does not lie in persecution and attack from *outside*. It lies in corruption *within* and the resultant degeneration. When the church is pure and strong in itself, it will of course make progress in favourable circumstances. But even when circumstances are unfavourable and the church is fiercely buffeted as by strong winds and violent rainstorms, it will only be purified and become more stable.

If the church is already corrupt within when it faces attacks from outside, there is no way to avoid ruin. Even when circumstances are favourable and the church appears outwardly to be flourishing, it will still be like the city of Babylon awaiting God's destruction.

Alas! Many believers have not yet even begun to awaken to these dangers. And even those who have awakened to these inner dangers are too fearful of giving offence and of embarrassing people. Considering their own interests, they are unwilling to speak out plainly; indeed, they dare not speak out plainly. In spite of these inner dangers, church leaders as well as the body of believers still live as if drunken and die as if in a dream. (19)

Brothers, if someone is caught in a sin, you who are spiritual should restore him gently. But watch yourself, or you also may be tempted.   **Galatians 6:1**

Those who sin are to be rebuked publicly, so that the others may take warning.   **1 Timothy 5:20**

In the name of the Lord Jesus Christ, we command you, brothers, to keep away from every brother who is idle and does not live according to the teaching you received from us.   **2 Thessalonians 3:6**

The Holy Spirit taught the church through the apostles how she should treat believers who were flagrantly sinning. As a first step, she should gently exhort them. If the offender is obdurate and proves irreclaimable, then she should rebuke him in the presence of the congregation. If he fails to respond to the rebuke and continues to sin, then the whole church should avoid him and break off fellowship with him.

What, we may ask, is the situation today? The large majority of churches have opened a big gulf between themselves and Christ; they have rejected his commands; they neither exhort nor rebuke those who have given themselves over to sin; still less do they rouse the whole church to avoid such people. As a consequence of this, there arises within the church a clique of those who are linked by their propensity to sin. Sometimes these people are not kept at arm's length; they may even be given high positions and exercise considerable authority within the church.

If this happens, weak believers are caused to stumble; those who have not yet repented may fall into all kinds of wickedness; and the church which bears Christ's name may become a lair of the devil. (19)

Woe to you, teachers of the law and Pharisees, you hypocrites! You clean the outside of the cup and dish, but inside they are full of greed and self-indulgence. Blind Pharisee! First clean the inside of the cup and dish, and then the outside also will be clean.

Matthew 23:25, 26

Let us now give consideration to those churches that have a name but lack the reality. They are indeed truly pitiful. Many of the prevalent sins in these churches are similar to those that are found in the world.

But there are two other kinds in addition. One of these is to be clearly aware of sin and yet deliberately to engage in it; the other is hypocrisy. When worldly people transgress, they may not realise that they are transgressing. But the same cannot be said of Christians. They are clearly aware that many things are acts of rebellion against God and are wrong yet they still reach the point of doing them. On the one hand, they acknowledge that these things are sinful and teach others that they are sinful; on the other hand, they still engage in these things.

How can this be explained? This is where the sin of hypocrisy comes in. The mouth is full of goodness and holiness, while the heart is full of unrighteousness and uncleanness. The appearance of these people in the sight of men is one thing; their appearance when out of sight is another. In guiding others, they habitually speak of devotion, righteousness, service and sacrifice but their own lives are full of vanity, self-seeking and avarice. In a loud voice they daily proclaim their love for the Lord and their love for people yet all the time they really only love themselves and their own interests. (2)

**I am jealous for you with a godly jealousy. I promised
you to one husband, to Christ, so that I might present
you as a pure virgin to him. But I am afraid that just as
Eve was deceived by the serpent's cunning, your minds
may somehow be led astray from your sincere and pure
devotion to Christ.   2 Corinthians 11:2, 3**

There is a sin of great gravity that exists in the church. It is
the sin of turning one's back on Christ and of committing
spiritual adultery with the world.

When individual believers commit adultery with the
world, they covet the wealth, benefits, glories and fame of the
world and turn their backs on Christ and his path of grace.

When a church as a whole commits adultery with the
world, it does everything possible to please the world and to
fall in with the currents of society; it abandons the gospel of
salvation and spreads materialistic concepts. By exploiting
the ability to engage in friendly intercourse, such a church
attracts people with wealth, education, reputation and
influence and in that way secures their help in material
matters. But because of this, they do not hesitate to accept
the guidance of these people and so are themselves drawn
into following the evil practices of the world. Thus the church
is completely transformed and becomes the residence of the
devil, the lair of unclean spirits, and a nest for all kinds of
hateful birds. Alas, that the church of Christ should become
so corrupted! Would it be strange if the wrath of God were
soon to descend on her and if, in a moment, she were to be
overturned? (2)

If anyone comes to you and does not bring this teaching, do not take him into your house or welcome him. Anyone who welcomes him shares in his wicked work.

                                     2 John 10, 11

With those who call themselves the servants of Christ but who neither spread the teaching of Christ nor obey it, we can have no kind of fellowship. Not only are we forbidden to receive them into our houses but we are also forbidden to welcome them. If we fail to follow this teaching and if we extend them a welcome, we partake of their wickedness.

One cannot think or speak of this without sighing. Few believers observe this teaching; very few are even aware that such a verse is found in Scripture.

We must hasten to repent before God. We must deal strictly with these wolves in sheep's clothing and with those who are prepared to betray Jesus for personal gain. In order to do this, we must be prepared to pay any price. People may say that we have no love; but we are not afraid of them saying that. People may criticise us, saying that we are proud and arrogant; but we are not afraid of that.

When we do what we do, we are simply following the teaching of Scripture. It is a case of our loving the Lord, loving the church and following the pattern that was set by our Lord Jesus Christ. It is a case of our seeking to hate sin as God does. It is simply a case of honouring God. (19)

But you, man of God, flee from all this, and pursue righteousness, godliness, faith, love, endurance and gentleness. Fight the good fight of faith.

                                      1 Timothy 6:11, 12

In the church today there are far too few people who are truly working for God. And even among those who are truly working for God, there are many whose lives embrace many things that call for reproof. Some lack chastity in relationships between men and women; some are insufficiently straightforward in matters relating to their possessions; some lack sincerity in both their words and their deeds; some are prone to be unjust in their treatment of other people.

Although these people enjoy a measure of success in their work, they fail to bear a good testimony in their lives. This not only means failure to stand firm in the face of their enemies, it also means that they lack the strength and courage that participation in spiritual warfare requires.

So long as conditions are favourable, they are able to take part in work that is not too demanding. But that is all that they can do. For when the day comes when they are plunged into fierce fighting and required to fight a good fight for truth, their life of defeat means that before they reach the battlefield their hearts are already cowed and frightened. Admittedly they do not fly the flag of surrender in the face of the enemy, but they cannot do other than beat a considerable retreat. Is there any hope of people like this winning a victory? (19)

**By the word of the Lord a man of God came from Judah
to Bethel . . . He cried out against the altar by the word
of the Lord . . . The altar was split apart and its ashes
poured out according to the sign given by the man of
God by the word of the Lord.   1 Kings 13:1–5**

A cloud of apostasy is spreading at the present time, all over
the world and all over the church. Everywhere you are faced
with examples of people burning incense on the altar of the
golden calf. It is one of the main tasks of preachers to speak
on behalf of God and to reprove wickedness, but when it
comes to it their mouths are closed and they are as silent as
the cicada in winter.

Among these preachers are those who do not dare to open
their mouths because they fear danger and disaster; those
who do not open their mouths because they want to secure
some benefit or gain; those who do not open their mouths
because they want to be in a position to please people or
excite their pity so that they can be sure of a livelihood, have
clothes to wear and satisfy themselves.

The need of the hour is for prophets who are not overawed
by power and influence, who do not fear danger, who do not
covet possessions, who do not pursue vainglory and who will
be prepared to stand up and speak for God. People like this
are vessels unto honour in the hand of God; they are pearls in
the church and they are lights in the world.

The church can do without the wealthy; the church can
do without those of high social position; the church can do
without able administrators; and the church can even do
without those who are gifted in preaching. But the church
cannot get along without those who are free from avarice and
fear. Only prophets like this can accomplish the will of God
and bring glory to God's holy name. (13)

The old prophet answered, 'I too am a prophet, as you are. And an angel said to me by the word of the Lord: "Bring him back with you to your house so that he may eat bread and drink water."' (But he was lying to him.)

1 Kings 13:18

Throughout the ages there have always been prophets who have fallen like this old prophet (1 Kings 13:11–32). They have previously been used by God and they have passed on the words of God. In course of time, as their years increase and their experiences multiply, they ought logically to become more useful and more helpful to other people. Unfortunately, through love of the world and because they have become carnally minded, they have in the end become degenerate. They no longer dare to rebuke evil; they no longer dare to oppose apostasy; even less do they dare to offend people. It is to be feared that as a consequence of this degeneration, they damage their own reputation, standing, interests and happiness.

Their fear of danger or disaster increases. As time goes on, they gradually lose their power and their testimony until these are gone entirely. They become careless about their work and they are only concerned to protect their own reputation, possessions, enjoyment and security. They no longer pay proper attention to God's commands and God's work. Their affections are taken over by their own fleshly appetites and it is to these that they pander. This is how they love themselves and those who are the objects of their love. Degenerate prophets like this are not only incapable of helping people, they are also, on the contrary, the means by which many are ruined. (13)

Month 2: Day 18   **Beware of self-proclaimed prophets**

The old prophet answered, 'I too am a prophet, as you are.'   **1 Kings 13:18**

Let us pay careful attention to a potentially very harmful and very dangerous statement that occurs in the words of the old prophet. 'I too am a prophet, as you are,' he said.

There are many Christians today who have suffered harm through statements like this. In all their previous contacts and associations with unbelievers, they have maintained an attitude of cautious fear and trembling. But the day comes when they encounter those who, like themselves, are Christians and they then relax. They cease to be watchful and no longer take necessary precautions. They do not realise that the Christians whom they have now encountered are degenerate Christians. Some of them are even counterfeit Christians. Before meeting these degenerate Christians, they had neither stumbled nor transgressed, even though they had had contact with unbelievers. It is only now that they are associating with so-called Christians that, contrary to all expectation, they stumble and fall into sin. These are occurrences that I have seen and heard all too frequently.

'I also am a Christian, as you are.' 'I also am a servant of God as you are.' I cannot estimate how many believers, lacking in watchfulness, have been hindered and harmed by words like these. So when we hear people with whom we are not well acquainted utter words like this, we ought to be particularly watchful. On no account must we lightly believe what they say. (13)

'With what shall I come before the Lord and bow down before the exalted God? Shall I come before him with burnt offerings, with calves a year old? Will the Lord be pleased with thousands of rams, with ten thousand rivers of oil? Shall I offer my firstborn for my transgression, the fruit of my body for the sin of my soul? He has showed you, O man, what is good. And what does the Lord require of you? To act justly and to love mercy and to walk humbly with your God.' Micah 6:6–8

In the church of the present day there are many believers who are just like the stubborn and perverse Israelites. There are even leaders in the church who are just like the hypocritical Pharisees.

They teach people to maintain their worship; they exhort people to increase their giving; they train people to sing melodious hymns; and they preach on themes related to prayer. At the same time, they observe that many believers are infected with all kinds of sin and cravings for that which is impure.

But they don't utter a single word of rebuke or warning, or call on the transgressors to repent and abandon their sin. Even less do they endeavour to lead them along the path of justice, compassion and sincerity. When they see a believer regularly attending worship and making large offerings, they regard him as a zealous believer but they do not enquire as to whether he has repented of his sin and diligently seeks to do God's will.

If leaders in the church are guilty of turning things upside down in this way, then it is not surprising that the believers in the flock whom they shepherd will reject the important things and choose the trivial ones. The Lord Jesus in his day reproved the hypocritical Pharisees. If he came today, would he not severely censure many leaders? (16)

Let us stop passing judgment on one another.   Romans 14:13

All our actions as individuals will one day be judged by the Lord. Only the Lord has authority to judge us. If anyone judges his brother, then he is acting on his own responsibility and taking over the Lord's authority. The sin of judging others may be trivial, but to overstep one's duty and to take over the Lord's authority is extremely grave.

In Romans 14:10–12 we find other teaching of the utmost gravity. 'We will all stand before God's judgment seat' and 'each of us will give an account of himself to God.' The apostle made these two statements specifically to remind us not to forget our own affairs. He wants us to ponder the words: 'We must all appear before the judgment seat of Christ, that each one may receive what is due to him for the things done while in the body, whether good or bad' (2 Corinthians 5:10).

If an individual believer really gave constant thought to the fact that he must one day stand before God's judgment seat, he would certainly not dare to judge other people any more. And if one who judges others could use his critical faculty to examine himself and judge himself, there would be no limit to the progress he would make and the blessing he would experience. (18)

As a prisoner for the Lord . . . I urge you to live a life worthy of the calling you have received.   Ephesians 4:1

Follow the way of love.   1 Corinthians 14:1

You must be very considerate of other people. Strive in every way to show them sympathy and to help them. Do not lightly become angry with those who are weaker than you or whose position is lower than yours. Do not shout or bawl at them. Do not put them in an embarrassing position. You should be large-hearted and magnanimous. No matter how people take advantage of you, do not be put out by it and do not allow it to rankle in your heart. Be forbearing towards people and be prepared to forgive them, just as God is forbearing and forgiving towards us.

Do not be easily shaken by the criticisms, judgments and slanders which people give vent to and do not demean yourself by speaking in these ways. On no account entertain the thought of raising yourself to a higher level than other people with a view to their according you honour. On the contrary, be willing to take a position lower than other people and look up to them with respect. Only those who are willing to take a lower position than other people are worthy to stand in a higher position.

If you yourself have a fault, you should confess it frankly; on no account think of ways to cover it up. When people reprove and exhort you, receive what they say in an attitude of humility and thankfulness. On no account reject their advice in anger.

Whenever there is an opportunity to obtain some benefit, let others go ahead to take advantage of it; but where there is danger or trouble, be ready yourself to go ahead and face it. (5)

Do not withhold good from those who deserve it, when it is in your power to act. Do not say to your neighbour, 'Come back later; I'll give it tomorrow' – when you now have it with you.   **Proverbs 3:27, 28**

The sluggard craves and gets nothing, but the desires of the diligent are fully satisfied ... Dishonest money dwindles away, but he who gathers money little by little makes it grow.   **Proverbs 13:4, 11**

Do not be afraid to lend things to other people, but do not lend them in a haphazard way. Being afraid to make loans to other people is to be selfish but to make loans haphazardly is to inflict harm on them. Never lend money to those who are lazy and unwilling to work. Do not lend money to people with bad habits. Do not lend money to those who tell lies and deceive people. If someone wants to borrow money from you in order to speculate with it, do not accede to his request. If people want to borrow money from you in order to spend it profligately – to buy ornate garments or give lavish feasts for friends or buy articles of luxury – do not respond to them.

But if people need money as a matter of urgency, so long as you have the means to help them, do not hold back. To relieve people in distress and be compassionate is the natural duty of Christians. When people who are in trouble or in distressing circumstances, or who have no strength to help themselves, seek to borrow money from you, you should not hold back. In fact, you should not expect to be repaid. Even less should you require interest.

If people want to borrow from you and you perceive that you cannot agree to do this, then be sincere in explaining the reason clearly. You should also take the opportunity to exhort them and not concoct excuses to explain your unwillingness to lend. Never lend money that has been entrusted to your care. It does not belong to you. (6)

**All of you, live in harmony with one another; be
sympathetic, love as brothers, be compassionate and
humble. Do not repay evil with evil or insult with insult,
but with blessing, because to this you were called so that
you may inherit a blessing.**   **1 Peter 3:8, 9**

In the treatment that you have received from other people,
there are beneficial features and there are also harmful
features. When you ponder the beneficial ways in which you
have been treated, your heart will be full of thanksgiving and
joy. Moreover you make many people your friends; you love
other people and other people love you.

But if you ponder the hurtful ways in which you have been
treated, your heart will be full of grief and hostility. Moreover
you will regard people as your enemies; and if you have an
aversion to other people, other people will have an aversion
to you.

When a person's life is overflowing with joy, not only is he
himself happy but he also makes other people happy. When a
person's life is overflowing with grief, not only is he himself
unhappy but he also makes other people unhappy. The
whole situation is determined by our attitudes.

Once we comprehend this reasoning, we should forget
the hurtful ways in which people have treated us and think
only of the beneficial ways in which they have treated us.
Admittedly, some people have treated us almost 100 per cent
hurtfully but even if there is only half a per cent of good in
their treatment, ought we not to focus on that and forget the
nearly 100 per cent of bad? Anyone who can attain this
standard is to be numbered among the wisest people in the
world. (17)

Month 2: Day 24   The interests of others

Each of you should look not only to your own interests, but also to the interests of others.   **Philippians 2:4**

Do everything in love.   **1 Corinthians 16:14**

When a person's disposition is that of self-seeking it is by no means easy to bring about a change so that he habitually seeks the well-being and interests of other people. It is necessary for him to keep close to God all the time and continuously to breathe in his love and power. He must also set his mind to rectify his normally selfish disposition and learn, in every way, to seek the interests of others and consider and help them.

It goes without saying that none of us should ever be the cause of other people suffering harm. We should avoid doing anything that causes grief and sorrow to others, anything that is a burden or stumbling-block to them – in short, anything that would be against their interests.

We ought, on the contrary, to lessen the suffering of other people and add to their joys. We should comfort the sorrowing and try to provide for people's needs. When it is a case of obtaining benefits, we should let others go ahead, and when it is a case of facing danger we should let others come behind us. When we have cause to rejoice, we should share our joy with others and when other people are called upon to suffer, we should share the taste of their bitterness with them.

But how shall we achieve all these things? It will require very great love, very great self-denial and very great sacrifice. But in the end we shall augment the happiness of other people and bring glory to God. At the same time, we will win wide respect. (17)

Naaman and all his attendants went back to the man of God. He stood before him and said, 'Now I know that there is no God in all the world except in Israel. Please accept now a gift from your servant.'   2 Kings 5:15, 16

Notice how Elisha sought neither to please nor to flatter Naaman, and how he damped Naaman's ardour and gave him guidance so that in the end he humbled himself (2 Kings 5). It truly causes us to look up to this prophet.

Notice again that after Naaman had bathed in the river and been cleansed, he returned to Elisha and begged him to accept the gifts that he had brought. But, although Naaman urged him repeatedly to accept these, Elisha refused, from beginning to end, to do so. This episode surely makes us respect Elisha enormously. He not only refrained from seeking gifts from Naaman but also, even when Naaman had gone out of his way to bring gifts to him, he was adamant in his refusal to accept them. Elisha's freedom from avarice and his self-discipline may justly be described as perfect.

But it was not really strange that Elisha, in the will of God, could show the way to Naaman so that in the end he humbled himself and became the recipient of God's grace. Only those who are free from avarice have the ability to refrain from flattering people and paying court to them. So long as a person harbours avarice in his heart, no matter how he aspires to chastity, what he seeks will be beyond him. No matter how watchful he is externally, it is out of the question for him to achieve anything worthwhile. In order to be notable in his manner of life, as Elisha was, a person must first of all be free from avarice, as Elisha was. (13)

A new commandment I give you: Love one another. As I have loved you, so you must love one another. All men will know that you are my disciples if you love one another.   **John 13:34, 35**

In any alliance of believers or in any fellowship among believers, nothing is of greater importance than mutual love. Yet nothing is more easily ruined than mutual love. Let there be even the tiniest impression of suspicion, a single malicious voice, the slightest sign of disrespect, or a few sentences of rumour – any of these are enough to light the fuse. If steps are not taken immediately to extinguish the burning fuse, any of these things are capable – sooner or later – of destroying this most valuable possession.

Since we are aware of this danger, we ought to be constantly watchful; we ought never to entertain a suspicion lightly; we ought to prohibit our lips from uttering words of malice about other people; we ought to maintain continually an attitude of humility; and we ought never to lend credence lightly to rumours we hear about people.

When we inadvertently give offence to people, we ought to seek their forgiveness. Should any brother treat me badly, I ought to forgive him in the same spirit as that in which God has forgiven me and not cherish the memory of his wrongdoing. When I observe that a brother has shortcomings, I ought to bear in mind that I have shortcomings too. Of even more importance is it that I should be perfectly sincere in all my dealings with others and that I am willing, in any matter, to suffer a disadvantage or even an injustice.

Only if we act like this, are we truly showing the mind of Christ. Only thus do we satisfy the Lord and only thus do we benefit other believers. In the end, this will also benefit us. (17)

**Do not use your freedom to indulge the sinful nature;
rather serve one another in love . . . If you keep on biting
and devouring each other, watch out or you will be
destroyed by each other.**   **Galatians 5:13, 15**

Love needs nourishment. For only then can it grow and
develop. To put it another way, if you do not nourish love and
if, on the contrary, you add that which is destructive, it is
liable to decay.

There are many genuine believers who have received the
life of God and who thereby inherit love. But – alas! – they do
not know how to cultivate the tender sprouts of this newly-
born love. On the contrary, through pride and arrogance,
through looking down on other people, through criticising
one another, through sustaining an attitude of suspicion,
through creating dissension and forming parties and through
envy and hatred, they perversely bring about the destruction
of these tender sprouts of love.

As a consequence, although they belong to Christ, when it
comes down to it, they do not possess the badge or marks of a
Christian. As a result of this, the world does not recognise
them as the disciples of Christ. Even though the Lord has
loved them and given his life for them, they still cannot love
one another as he commanded and, on the contrary, bite and
devour each other. Naturally the Lord is conscious of in-
expressible grief and sadness. The disciples themselves also
fail to enjoy the benefits of loving one another. What a
lamentable situation this is! (17)

Dear friends, let us love one another, for love comes from God. Everyone who loves has been born of God and knows God. Whoever does not love does not know God, because God is love.   1 John 4:7, 8

In the process of learning this lesson of loving one another, there is one important principle to which we must pay close attention: each of us ought to do our utmost to love people, but we ought not to plan to gain other people's love. By all means let us regard loving other people as a duty but when other people love us, let us regard it as a favour.

When believers in general give thought to the Lord's teaching about loving one another, they almost invariably assume that they ought to be loved by other people. Their attitude may be expressed like this: Since the Lord teaches us to love one another, then *you* ought to love me, *you* ought to forgive me, *you* ought to help me, *you* ought to serve me and *you* ought to come to my aid when I am in difficulty.

But when those who truly love the Lord give thought to his teaching that we should love one another, their attitude ought to be this: *I* ought to love other people, *I* ought to forgive other people, *I* ought to help other people, *I* ought to serve other people and *I* ought to help other people when they are in difficulty. If, however, other people love me and help me, I regard this as grace, and I ought to give thanks for it.

If every believer thought only in terms of being loved by other people, then the exhortation to love one another would have no means of expression. But if every believer thought in terms of loving other people, the teaching that we should love one another would immediately become a reality. It follows that the church would then be filled with the spirit of mutual love. (17)

This is love: not that we loved God, but that he loved us and sent his Son as an atoning sacrifice for our sins. Dear friends, since God so loved us, we also ought to love one another.   1 John 4:6, 11

In what manner did the Lord love us? It was not only when we were good that he loved us; he still loved us when we were bad. When we quarrelled as to who was the greatest he did not reprove us but he bent down to wash our feet. When we swore on oath that we did not know him, he did not complain about us but turned and looked at us. When we doubted him, he did not cast us off but pointed to the nail-prints in his hands and the wound-marks in his side. He loves us all today in the same way that he loved his disciples when he was on earth.

In what way, then, are we disciples to love one another? He teaches us that we ought to love one another not only when we have in mind people's good points and excellences but also when we have in mind each other's shortcomings and inferiorities; in exactly the same way as the Lord loved us even when he perceived our shortcomings and depravity. For us to love one another in this way is not by any means easy. But when we ponder how the Lord loved us, we will want to go and do likewise. (17)

Fathers, do not exasperate your children; instead, bring them up in the training and instruction of the Lord.
                        Ephesians 6:4

Those who are parents must set an example for their children in both words and deeds and in their whole manner of life.

You must guide and instruct your children to fear God, to believe in the Lord Jesus, to study diligently, to work faithfully, to be sincere and void of hypocrisy and to be sympathetic to others. You must help your children so that their faith and virtue alike are established on firm foundations.

If you observe faults in your children, on no account ignore them, and on no account refrain from asking questions, for such neglect can easily lead to their ruin.

Do not accumulate large sums of money for your children or purchase large properties for them.

There may be times when you are unhappy or when there is friction between you and other people. On those occasions, be sure that you do not work out your reactions on your children – losing your temper with them, rebuking them unnecessarily or even striking them.

If in any matter you take advantage of your children, you ought to acknowledge your faults to them in all sincerity. To acknowledge one's faults is an act of nobility.

What attitude should you adopt when someone speaks to you about the faults of your children? You should express your thanks and accept what they say. For if people are willing to do this, it demonstrates their loyalty to you and their sincerity. It also shows their love for both you and your children. (15)

**Wives, submit to your husbands as to the Lord. For the
husband is the head of the wife as Christ is the head of
the church, his body, of which he is the Saviour ...
Husbands, love your wives, just as Christ loved the
church and gave himself up for her.**

Ephesians 5:22, 23, 25

**Children, obey your parents in the Lord, for this is right
... Fathers, do not exasperate your children; instead,
bring them up in the training and instruction of the
Lord.**   **Ephesians 6:1, 4**

When many believers read these passages, they make a
profound mistake. They fail to stress the particular passages
that God addresses to them; they only stress the parts that
God addresses to others.

Those who are wives do not stress the fact that they ought
to submit to their husbands; they only stress that husbands
ought to love their wives. Similarly husbands do not stress
the way that they ought to love their wives but only that
wives ought to submit to their husbands.

Children ignore the teaching that they ought to be filial
and obey their parents; they only know that they want their
parents to treat them according to God's will. Parents, on the
other hand, neglect what this passage says about their duties
towards their children and habitually upbraid their children,
requiring them to be filial and obedient.

Each individual neglects his or her own particular duties
while expecting others to be dutiful. What God desires is that
we pay particular attention to the instructions that relate
specifically to us. As for the things that others ought to carry
out, we should leave those for *them* to stress. (17)

Isaac, who had a taste for wild game, loved Esau, but Rebekah loved Jacob.   **Genesis 25:28**

When his brothers saw that their father loved him more than any of them, they hated him and could not speak a kind word to him.   **Genesis 37:4**

In the first story, the father loved his first-born son and sought to shower upon him all kinds of privileges. But the mother loved the second son and sought therefore to obtain many blessings for him. Isaac had the authority to bless Esau but Rebekah was sufficiently cunning to help Jacob to tell a lie and, by cheating, to obtain the blessing for him.

The fact is, no matter how many children parents have, they should treat them all alike. On no account should the situation arise in which the father has a special love for this one while the mother has a special love for that one. Such a situation inevitably leads to the formation of parties – the father with one of the children on one side and the mother with another child on the other side.

If there happen to be other children in the family who are denied the love and favour of their parents, they will become prodigals. They will find fault and sow the seeds of dissension and the home will soon become a battlefield.

Even if both parents are specially drawn to the same child, the situation is equally undesirable and dissension is bound to arise. The end result can only be disastrous. And even if the child who is specially loved does not wish to be a favourite, the other children will still envy him and come to hate him. As time goes on, such situations grow more and more serious. (17)

Jesus declared, 'I tell you the truth, unless a man is born again, he cannot see the kingdom of God.'   **John 3:3**

If the root of a tree is dried up, of what use is it to try to improve the leaves? If the spring is muddy, is it not a waste of time to try and purify the stream?

God does not do stupid things like that. The method he uses is to correct the source and purify the spring. He is aware that the inability of people to do good is an inner question and not an external one; it is a question of life rather than, merely, conduct. Because of this, he does not instruct us to improve our old life, which is already corrupt, by human methods. He simply says to us, 'You must be born again!'

His meaning is plain: Your old life is the source of all your sins; your old life can never be repaired; your old life can never be good; your old life can never satisfy me. I now announce a remedy that is basic. I intend that you should receive a new life entirely. Once you have received this new life, you will hate sin and it will certainly be your desire to do good. Only then can you enter my kingdom, and only then will you be pleasing to me. In view of all these considerations I now declare to you, 'You must be born again!' (3)

The wind blows wherever it pleases. You hear its sound, but you cannot tell where it comes from or where it is going. So it is with everyone born of the Spirit.   John 3:8

What are the signs of the new birth? Certain special phenomena are immediately apparent in one who is born again. There is an unprecedented transformation of his whole being. His thoughts, his purposes, his hopes, his words, his conduct – in fact, his whole manner of life – are all changed.

Whereas he was once inclined to sin, he now takes his stand against sin. Whereas he once desired to be commended by men, he now welcomes their rebuke and correction. Whereas he was once self-seeking, he now loves other people like himself. Whereas he once hankered after the pleasures of the world, he now pursues heavenly ambitions. Whereas he once had no time for the Bible, the Bible is now his delight.

Those who once sought worldly friends, now look for their friends among believers. Those who were once far from God and slandered him, have now become those who put their trust in God, worship him and zealously serve him.

These changes are all of vital importance: inner changes of the heart and changes relating to life. Only fundamental changes of this nature can serve to demonstrate that a person is truly born again. (3)

Month 3: Day 5   There must be some evidence!

The wind blows wherever it pleases. You hear its sound, but you cannot tell where it comes from or where it is going. So it is with everyone born of the Spirit.   John 3:8

One spring morning, I was sitting with a friend on the top of a hill surveying the country around. I observed that the water in the lake was as smooth as a mirror; neither in the leaves on the trees nor in the grass was there the slightest sign of movement. I could see a tower in the distance on which a flag was draped motionless around the flagpole and it was impossible to discern what the flag was. No dust whatever could be seen blowing on the roads and, apart from the chirping of a few small birds, there was not the slightest sound to be heard. It was a scene of perfect tranquillity.

Suddenly my friend opened his mouth and remarked to me: 'Fancy the wind blowing as strongly as this!'

Listening to his words, I couldn't be other than absolutely amazed. It is true that the wind and its actual blowing cannot be discerned by human eyes. Nevertheless, whenever the wind is blowing there will, without question, be phenomena produced by this; and only because of such phenomena can we be certain that the wind is blowing at any given moment.

The same holds true when a person is born again of the Spirit. Unless I can see at least some slight effect of the blowing of the wind, I can by no means believe that the wind is blowing. In the same way, if we cannot see even a slight manifestation of the new birth, how can we believe that the person concerned has been born again? (3)

Just as Moses lifted up the snake in the desert, so the Son of Man must be lifted up, that everyone who believes may have eternal life in him.   **John 3:14, 15**

The Lord Jesus used the event referred to in John 3:14, 15 to guide Nicodemus and to show him the way in which a person is born again. He told Nicodemus that, like the Israelites, the whole human race had sinned and encountered God's anger and forfeited their lives. And just as the Israelites who had forfeited their lives received new life when they lifted up their eyes to the serpent of brass, so those who have forfeited their lives today receive new life when they put their trust in the Lord Jesus.

Here is a clear answer to the question: How can a person be born again? It is simply by believing in the Lord Jesus Christ, who, by his death on the cross, has already accomplished the work of salvation. All that is now necessary is that we genuinely repent of our sin and wholeheartedly put our trust in the Lord Jesus, who laid down his life for us. We are saved immediately; we are born again; we have eternal life.

Have you believed in this way? If you have done so, you can be assured that you have been born again and that you have eternal life. (3)

My dear children, I write this to you so that you will not sin. But if anybody does sin, we have one who speaks to the Father in our defence – Jesus Christ, the Righteous One. He is the atoning sacrifice for our sins, and not only for ours but also for the sins of the whole world.

1 John 2:1, 2

This passage is written for those who are already born again. John announces that what he writes to them is in order that they might not sin. If it were not possible for them to sin, these verses would not have been necessary. It is written to help them not to sin. But unfortunately there are those who still sin, so what about them?

'If anybody does sin, we have one who speaks to the Father in our defence – Jesus Christ, the Righteous One. He is the atoning sacrifice for our sins.' What a precious promise this is!

In what way, we may ask, can these words be of help to those believers who have been wounded by sin? How can it comfort them and prevent them from being discouraged or from despairing? The fact is, if every believer kept these words clearly in mind, then a vast amount of suffering, fear, despondency and despair would be avoided. No true believers would take these words as licence to go and sin at will. The gracious words in this passage are what God has given to his children to help them in a time of weakness and sin. (3)

When I want to do good, evil is right there with me.
Romans 7:1

The apostle Paul relates the struggle he experienced after he had been born again (Romans 7:14–24). Many born-again believers in our own day find an echo in their own hearts of what Paul describes here. They experience a conflict of this kind; they encounter this kind of defeat; they suffer similar pain.

Once we understand the nature of the conflict between the new man and the old man, we realise that when believers are thrown into a fierce battle of this kind, it is not to be regarded as evidence that they have not been born again. It is evidence, on the contrary, that they *are* born again. They suffer bitter defeat because the strength of the inner being is not strong enough to overcome the outer being. When the inner being gains control, the believer lives a life of holiness and joy and satisfaction. But when the outer being is in control, the life of the believer is polluted, depraved, troubled and distressing.

In Paul's letter to the church at Ephesus he wrote: 'I kneel before the Father, from whom the whole family in heaven and on earth derives its name. I pray that out of his glorious riches he may strengthen you with power through his Spirit in your inner being' (Ephesians 3:15, 16). This is the prayer that Paul offered up for the church. It should be a petition that we all offer up in the presence of God. (3)

The Pharisees . . . asked his disciples, 'Why does your teacher eat with tax collectors and "sinners"?' On hearing this, Jesus said . . . 'I have not come to call the righteous, but sinners.'   Matthew 9:11–13

When they kept on questioning him, he straightened up and said to them, 'If any one of you is without sin, let him be the first to throw a stone at her.'   John 8:7

He said, 'Jesus, remember me when you come into your kingdom.' Jesus answered him, 'I tell you the truth, today you will be with me in paradise.'   Luke 23:42, 43

Who among us can be reckoned as superior to the sinners, tax-gatherers and adulterers mentioned in these passages? Admittedly we may not have acquired anything dishonestly or acted unreasonably to profit ourselves while involving others in loss or had any liaison with people of the opposite sex other than our partners. But in the sight of God are we really upright and pure? Haven't our thoughts been evil – embracing avarice, hate, envy and licentiousness?

When we human beings look at each other, we see only the outward appearance but what God looks at is the heart. Whether a person's courage is great or small, whether he is thin-skinned or thick-skinned, whether he has been strictly brought up or not – these things, together with the situation in the home, are closely connected with his character and conduct. The flesh in all of us is corrupt and evil; the hearts of all men are deceitful; but because of differing circumstances people's characters and standards of virtue vary tremendously.

Yet in the sight of God all men are equally sinners and all men are equally corrupt. No one stands higher than another. No one has authority to reject another. No one has authority to condemn the sin of others. (14)

Jesus answered him, 'I tell you the truth, today you will be with me in paradise.'   **Luke 23:43**

Though my father and mother forsake me, the Lord will receive me.   .   **Psalm 27:10**

The Lord is willing to receive those whom the world is unwilling to receive. Think of the robber who was saved on the cross. Who else except the Lord was willing to have compassion on him and help him? No one at all. It was the one whom the people hated – the Lord himself – who received him.

There are probably two reasons for people being unwilling to repent. First, they have not yet become aware of their wickedness so they see no need to repent. Second, they have a feeling that their sins are so great that the Lord cannot be both able and willing to forgive them. But it is not true that the Lord is unwilling to forgive their sins.

If you have doubts on this point, think for a moment of the robber. It may be that your sins are so grave that you have lost the respect of other people and been forsaken by your parents; that when you go to a place of worship you are specially noticed and those who know you are unwilling to talk to you. These things may indeed be true but I want to tell you this: without any question, the Lord is still willing to receive you; he wants to bestow that great and marvellous salvation of his on all those whom the world is unwilling to receive. (4)

I give them eternal life, and they shall never perish; no one can snatch them out of my hand.   John 10:28

The two promises in this verse are a source of great comfort to us. They assure us that our salvation is accomplished once for all and also that it is determined for all eternity.

There are not a few believers who believe that they have received eternal life and yet, at the same time, they are never free from the fear that if they are weak or stumble or fail or backslide – then their eternal life may be in jeopardy.

Yet what the Lord bestows upon us is eternal life, and the very expression means that it cannot be lost. If we are capable of losing the life that has been bestowed upon us, then it cannot be called eternal life. And how much stronger this declaration becomes when we read what the Lord so clearly states: 'They shall never perish.'

Brothers and sisters! You who have truly believed in the Lord! Do not doubt the Lord's promise any longer! Never again be afraid that having once been saved you can forfeit the life you have received. Such a thing is totally impossible. Once a sinner has repented and put his trust in the Lord, he is saved immediately. He has eternal life and is saved for ever – he will for ever possess the life that God bestows on him. And that life is called eternal life. (14)

The God of peace be with you all. Amen.　Romans 15:33

We all ought to be aware that peace is derived from the God of peace. If you worship God, trust in God, obey God and draw near to God, then you will have peace. If you envisage no God, if you are the enemy of God or are far from God, then you will not enjoy peace. So when we sin we cannot enjoy peace. Sin and God cannot exist together. It is sin that separates us from God; it is God who separates us from sin. So long as we do not keep our distance from sin, we shall remain far from God. But when we draw near to God and distance ourselves from sin, we shall have peace. On the other hand, when we keep close to sin and draw away from God, we shall lose our peace. The more we sin, the further we are from peace.

If you have no ambition to enjoy peace, then so be it. But if you are hoping to obtain peace, the one and only way is first to confess sin and turn away from sin and with your whole heart return to God.

After that, you should use all your strength to persuade other people to abandon their sins and seek to lead them to God. For every single individual who abandons his sin and turns to God, there is one unit less of misery in the world and one unit more of the sum total of peace in the world. (13)

Make every effort to keep the unity of the Spirit through the bond of peace.   **Ephesians 4:3**

Being united as one is the state that the Lord Jesus sought from God for his disciples. Paul also, in his letters, earnestly exhorted the church to preserve unity.

However, there is one point that we must clearly understand. Being united as one does not refer to believers and unbelievers becoming one nor to the church and the world becoming one. The Bible consistently teaches the church that it ought to be one but it also reminds believers that they must distance themselves from false brothers who resist the truth and from those who contaminate the church.

Clearly then, being united as one does not mean that believers are to be one with the unbelieving faction or with loose-living counterfeit believers. Those who belong to the Lord ought to separate from these people. Only those who belong to the Lord can be united in love. For it is only as they have the same faith, the same purposes, the same hopes and the same objectives that they can be united as one. This is not only what *ought* to be; this is also what *can* be. (19)

The messenger who had gone to summon Micaiah said to him, 'Look, as one man the other prophets are predicting success for the king. Let your word agree with theirs, and speak favourably.' But Micaiah said, 'As surely as the Lord lives, I can tell him only what the Lord tells me.'   **1 Kings 22:13, 14**

The words that this messenger addressed to Micaiah were uttered with good intentions. But what did Micaiah reply? 'As surely as the Lord lives, I can tell him only what the Lord tells me.' Absolutely right! This and only this is the attitude that the servant of God ought to adopt: not in any way swayed by powers and authorities and not in any way bound by the ideas of men. Only in this way can one be a good servant of God.

It is just at this point that many servants of God are found to fail. Their parents, their wives, their brothers and sisters, their friends and others address them with beguiling words like this: Other preachers all say things that please the ear; none of them provoke people's wrath. Why do you alone persist in rebuking people? Why do you point out people's shortcomings and warn of coming disasters? Preaching of this nature will only call forth opposition and attack. So why do you not speak in the same manner as others do and concentrate on auspicious words as they do?

Many of those who work for God have been moved by specious arguments like these. Half way along the road, they have lost their singleness of purpose and undergone a change of heart. As a consequence, they have been thrown over by God for God can no longer use them. Preachers who have succumbed in this way, both past and present, are too numerous to count.

My brothers and sisters! You are my fellow-workers in the service of the Lord. Let us keep a watch on ourselves! (12)

The king of Israel then ordered, 'Take Micaiah and send him back to Amon the ruler of the city and to Joash the king's son and say "This is what the king says: Put this fellow in prison and give him nothing but bread and water until I return safely."'   **1 Kings 22:26, 27**

Here we see a loyal prophet, who spoke for God, being humiliated and beaten by his fellows and, on top of that, being thrown into prison by the king. There he suffered, having neither enough to eat nor enough to drink.

Yet what did all that matter? It is true that he was badly treated for a while but, through this, he received great reward in the sight of God; and all who suffer persecution for the sake of Christ will receive a great reward in heaven.

The world daily gets worse. The church becomes more and more corrupt. The majority turn their backs on God; most of them practise unrighteousness; they are stubborn and rebellious; they run full tilt into disaster. If only there were ten or a hundred or a thousand prophets like Micaiah to come to the fore and utter inauspicious words!

O God! For the sake of the world today, and for the sake of the church today, we plead with you to raise up a few more prophets who speak inauspicious words. (12)

Therefore, I declare to you today that I am innocent of the blood of all men. For I have not hesitated to proclaim to you the whole will of God.   **Acts 20:26, 27**

This is the commission that God's servants receive from God – to proclaim the whole will of God. Those who have abandoned this mission are basically unworthy to continue to be called God's servants.

Sometimes, when a believer listens to a preacher who accurately speaks of certain sins of which he is guilty, he thinks that the preacher is purposely humiliating him and attacking him. As a consequence, he shows his dissatisfaction with the preacher concerned.

Some preachers seek to ward off this kind of opposition and do all they can to avoid wounding the feelings of their congregation. As a result, many truths are not preached and many sins are not rebuked. This means, in turn, that the themes selected for sermons are often totally unrelated either to the faith or to the Christian life. In this way, preachers avoid creating enemies. Yet in the sight of God they lose their usefulness entirely and it is inevitable that they are then discarded by him.

Those who work for God must make up their minds. When it comes down to it, what is their aim – to please God or to please men? It is impossible to follow both of these roads at the same time and they must make their choice. (11)

Going a little farther, he fell with his face to the ground and prayed, 'My Father, if it is possible, may this cup be taken from me. Yet not as I will, but as you will.'

                                                    Matthew 26:39

Without any doubt whatever, whenever our Lord dealt with any problem or handled any matter of business, the criterion to which he turned was this: Is it or is it not the will of God?

Before we are enveloped in a particular battle, we must be fully prepared and establish the attitude of seeking only the will of God. We are not to be taken up with questions of our benefit or harm, our profit or loss, our glory or shame, our being cursed or blessed, our happiness or misery, our peace or danger and even our life or death. If by doing the will of God we ensure a brilliant future, we naturally would wish to press boldly ahead; but even if by doing the will of God we court trouble for ourselves, we still do not hesitate or hold back. At any time, and in any place, we may sacrifice all we have, but what we must never do is disobey the will of God.

In dealing with all our problems and in facing the affairs of our lives, we ought to keep a firm grip on one principle: Don't ask whether it means profit or loss; only ask whether it is right or wrong. If it is in accordance with God's will, it is right; if it is not in accordance with God's will, it is wrong. This is the principle that our Lord followed throughout the whole of his life on earth. We who are his disciples should do the same. (11)

'The time has come,' he said. 'The kingdom of God is near. Repent and believe the good news!'   Mark 1:15

Peter replied, 'Repent and be baptised, every one of you, in the name of Jesus Christ so that your sins may be forgiven. And you will receive the gift of the Holy Spirit.'   Acts 2:38

It is a great pity that so many preachers preach the gospel in a debilitated way. They preach that in order for a person to be saved, he must believe in Jesus; but they do not preach the need for repentance. They have not led people to be aware of their own sins; even less have they called on people to confess their sins and to turn away from them. They preach the facts of Christ dying for men's sins; yet their listeners, because they have not become aware of their sins, still less confessed and repented of them, are naturally incapable of putting their trust in Jesus.

In these circumstances, if there are those who indicate their belief in Jesus, the best among them simply esteem the spirit of of Jesus in matters such as sacrificing one's life to preserve one's integrity and giving up the world to seek righteousness; or they may admire the noble virtues of Jesus and his great personality; but they don't realise that knowing the facts about Jesus is one thing and believing in Jesus is another.

We cannot be saved through simply knowing the facts about Jesus. We are saved through sincerely repenting and trusting in him. Many people are under the impression that simply because they know the facts about Jesus, they are believers in Jesus. It is even more lamentable that many preachers are also under this impression. (16)

There are six things the Lord hates, seven that are detestable to him: haughty eyes, a lying tongue, hands that shed innocent blood, a heart that devises wicked schemes, feet that are quick to rush into evil, a false witness who pours out lies and a man who stirs up dissension among brothers.   Proverbs 6:16−19

Blessed are the peacemakers, for they will be called sons of God.   Matthew 5:9

You who stir up strife! Do not depend on your own appraisals. The God who examines men's hearts has long known all your thoughts. He has also long ago heard those words of yours that stir up strife. The words I now quote apply to you: 'Men will have to give account on the day of judgment for every careless word they have spoken' (Matthew 12:36). Since words that you have spoken have stirred up strife, and ruined many people, of a certainty he will condemn you according to your words. When you utter words that stir up strife, it may seem as if the only harm they cause is to other people but you will discover that they also greatly harm yourself.

The Bible not only forbids us to utter words that stir up strife, it also teaches us to use words that promote harmony. 'God . . . reconciled us to himself through Christ and gave us the ministry of reconciliation' (2 Corinthians 5:18). Christians ought, first of all, to urge people to be reconciled to God. They ought, secondly, to urge people to be reconciled to one another.

By constantly using speech that promotes harmony we help to eliminate words that stir up strife and are enabled to obtain God's special promises. The Lord Jesus taught us that 'blessed are the peacemakers, for they will be called sons of God.' (18)

**This is what the Lord says: 'Let not the wise man boast of
his wisdom or the strong man boast of his strength or the
rich man boast of his riches, but let him who boasts boast
about this: that he understands and knows me, that I am
the Lord, who exercises kindness, justice and righteousness on earth, for in these I delight,' declares the
Lord.** **Jeremiah 9:23, 24**

**Young men . . . be submissive to those who are older.
Clothe yourselves with humility towards one another,
because, 'God opposes the proud but gives grace to the
humble.'** **1 Peter 5:5**

The use of boastful words is not easy to avoid. A person who
possesses certain strong points or merits has a tendency,
when opportunity offers, to use boastful expressions as a
means of engendering respect and commendation. There are
people who delight to boast but who do not easily have
opportunities to do so and therefore devise various ways of
displaying themselves.

Words in praise of oneself arise from pride. Those who are
given to bragging are undoubtedly haughty and arrogant in
their hearts, and underneath the surface lies the desire to
appropriate for themselves the glory that rightly belongs to
God. Because of this, they do not tell of the compassion and
love and power of God; instead of that, they consistently
display their own merits.

Presumptuous conduct of this kind is in the sight of God
extremely wicked. Thus when we read in the Bible of the
seven things that God abhors we find that 'haughty eyes' is
first on the list (Proverbs 6:16–19). God gives grace to the
humble, and thus raises him to glory, but the proud he brings
down to the ground. The best route to glory is to obey the
injunction in 1 Peter 5:6: 'Humble yourselves . . . under
God's mighty hand, that he may lift you up in due time.' (18)

Find out what pleases the Lord.   Ephesians 5:10

My heart is set on keeping your decrees to the very end.
                                   Psalm 119:112

When we have made up our mind that we will seek to please
God, we must take the truth of God as our sole arbiter in
determining the way we should live. So long as the things we
do are genuinely in accordance with his commands, we have
no need to enquire whether or not people praise us and
whether or not people speak well of us.

Not all the things that people regard as good are good in
the sight of God. It should be our ambition not that men
should speak well of us but that God should speak well of us.

There are some believers who are afraid that they will
dishonour God's name or cause God to be slandered, so they
strive all they can to act in ways that men acknowledge as
good. They are under the impression that if they can satisfy
the hopes of men, they can in that way cause the name of God
to be honoured. But in doing this, it is very easy for them to
concentrate their attention on men. As a consequence, there
may be an unconscious drift on their part towards following
the ideas of men and away from the will of God. (16)

A man's pride brings him low, but a man of lowly spirit gains honour.   **Proverbs 29:23**

It is the proud whom God most abhors. In the sight of God, the most abhorrent sin is pride. He is aware that haughty eyes are the source of sins of every kind. He is aware that as soon as people have haughty eyes, they may not only leave men but also God out of their consideration. God is aware that when people have haughty eyes they are capable of acting as they please, standing in awe of no one and indulging in unseemly behaviour. Consequently, when God sees people becoming proud, he seeks to bring them down from their high position.

God caused Uzziah, because of his pride, to contract leprosy and he became a leper until the day of his death. Because of Hezekiah's pride, God caused his family to be taken to Babylon. He caused the king of Assyria, because of his pride, to be destroyed; and he caused Nebuchadnezzar, because of his boasting, to be driven from among men and to eat grass like cattle: 'Seven times will pass by for you until you acknowledge that the Most High is sovereign over the kingdoms of men' (Daniel 4:25).

Whoever uplifts himself in the sight of God is himself provoking abasement; whoever is proud in the sight of God is bringing ruin on himself. To be proud in the sight of men is to be courting shame and no more. But to be proud in the sight of God will not only incur shame, it will also bring ruin. (17)

For who makes you different from anyone else? What do you have that you did not receive? And if you did receive it, why do you boast as though you did not?

1 Corinthians 4:7

What have we to be proud about? Which of our good points is not the product of God's grace? If he did not bestow his grace upon us, how could we work for him? If he did not bestow on us money and ability, what would we possess with which to do good? If he did not open our eyes, how would we recognise him? If he did not accomplish our salvation, how could we escape from sin and from the punishment of sin? If he did not give us a mind, how could we engage in thinking? If he did not give us life and breath, how could we even exist in the world?

All gifts and all benefits are derived from him; all our good deeds are what he himself performs through us. All that we could do ourselves was to rebel against God; we could only be transgressors; we were only capable of bringing disaster upon ourselves. Within us there was no good whatever: 'The heart is deceitful above all things and beyond cure, who can understand it?' (Jeremiah 17:9). What grounds for pride can there be in people like us? Those who know themselves are not proud; those who are proud do not know themselves. (17)

And now, Father, glorify me in your presence with the glory I had with you before the world began.   John 17:5

Jesus replied, 'If I glorify myself, my glory means nothing. My Father, whom you claim as your God, is the one who glorifies me.'   John 8:54

Our Lord did not seek glory from men; nor did he receive glory from men; but he did seek glory from God. He also loved and admired God's glory. Even more, he regarded the reception of God's glory as that which was most gratifying. This is how he once addressed his Father: 'And now, Father, glorify me in your presence with the glory I had with you before the world began.' In these words he directly asked the Father that he might enjoy glory with him.

Obviously, it is not wrong to seek glory. What *is* wrong is to seek glory from men rather than God. If we are seeking the glory of God, we will do all that we can to be pleasing to him and we will do the things that he has commanded us to do. But if we are seeking the glory of men, we will be doing all that we can to be pleasing to men and we will do the things that men want us to do. In those circumstances, we will not be able to avoid rebelling against God's commands. We will transgress in many ways, forfeiting the many blessings that God would bestow on us and also experiencing misfortune. (17)

And if I go and prepare a place for you, I will come back and take you to be with me that you also may be where I am.   **John 14:3**

In a successful marriage there must be fervent love between husband and wife. Where love like this exists, a husband does not pick out a few items from his assets and benefits and hand them over to his wife. He takes all that he has and places it before them both so that he and she may share everything.

Since the church is the future wife of Christ, the love with which he loves her is true and fervent. Therefore he takes all that he has and promises his bride that in the future they will both share it.

'That you also may be where I am.' What a precious promise this is! Christ has already ascended to heaven and is in the Father's house, one day to be revealed in glory and to reign as King. After his bride has been caught up, she will never again be separated from him. He will be with her in the Father's home, and with her at the marriage feast, afterwards being glorified and reigning with her on earth.

Once Christians are fully assured of the truth of this promise, they will abound in joy and comfort and hope. And what is more, will they not hold lightly to fleshly and transient pleasures and the merrymaking and entertainments of the world? (1)

**When the crowd saw what Paul had done, they shouted
in the Lycaonian language, 'The gods have come down
to us in human form!' . . . The crowd wanted to offer
sacrifices to them.**   Acts 4:11, 13

When a servant of God is manifestly used by him – such as
when Paul healed certain people's diseases or when Peter's
preaching moved people to repent and trust the Lord – many
zealous Christians are found hurrying to them and making
offerings to them. In other words, they excessively venerate
the servants of God.

But what happens when they become aware of shortcomings in the life of a servant of God whom they have been
venerating? It is as if a bucket of cold water had been thrown
over their faith. They hadn't expected that God's servants
would sin in the same way as ordinary believers. The thought
comes to them that if such people can fall into sin, what hope
is there for them? So they are caused to stumble and they lose
heart, overlooking the fact that it is only God who is entirely
free from shortcomings and incapable of committing sin. For
no matter how good God's servants may be, in the end they
are still human beings and no different in their make-up from
others. (16)

Men, why are you doing this? We too are only men, human like you. We are bringing you good news, telling you to turn from these worthless things to the living God.   **Acts 14:15**

Excessive veneration of the servants of God is dangerous because, while we are striving to copy their good points, we may also copy their shortcomings. Naturally those whom God greatly uses invariably have noticeable good points but, at the same time, because they are human beings, they cannot avoid having shortcomings. So those who emulate them may copy their shortcomings as well as their good points.

For example, if a person whom God uses is a humble seeker after truth, he may be used by God to edify many people in this way. But because he is also a man, he cannot be entirely free from prejudices. Those who are seeking to emulate him may see his prejudices as aspects of biblical truths.

In order to avert this danger, we must always bear in mind that those whom we admire and look up to are still human beings with dispositions like ours. They all have their shortcomings; they all have their faults. (16)

Jesus answered, 'I tell you the truth, you are looking for me, not because you saw miraculous signs but because you ate the loaves and had your fill. Do not work for food that spoils, but for food that endures to eternal life, which the Son of Man will give you. On him God the father has placed his seal of approval.'   John 6:26, 27

In the episode of Jesus distributing bread, we may discern a perfectly orthodox approach – that is, an emphasis on teaching about spiritual life accompanied by concern for the needs of the body. What Jesus always emphasised most of all was the preaching of the word. But having preached the word, he was also concerned that people should have enough food to eat. So on this occasion, he commanded the disciples to give the people food to eat. Jesus always regarded the preaching of the word as his most important work, but after that came the task of distributing food.

But there is more than that to be observed here. On one day, his work of preaching was followed by the preparation of food for the people. But on the next day, when the people went to seek him at Capernaum, he only preached the word to them, and did not go on to prepare food for them.

On the first day the people came in order to hear the preaching; and, because they listened to the preaching until evening, they had no means of going to buy bread, so Jesus prepared food for them to eat. But on the second day, the purpose for which they sought him was different. On that occasion, when they came to Capernaum it was not in order to listen to the preaching again; it was solely in order to eat and be filled. Jesus perceived this situation and adopted a different procedure from the first day and made no move to prepare food for them. (14)

Month 3: Day 29   Does God always will healing?

This is the assurance we have in approaching God: that if we ask anything according to his will, he hears us.
1 John 5:14

In the apostolic age, God manifested his great power and authority and, through the apostles and preachers of the gospel, healed many who were diseased. Naturally God can still operate in this way but the facts tell us that he does not *normally* do so.

The question arises: Are there instances of healing through prayer in our own generation? I can answer that question without any hesitation whatever: 'Yes, indeed!' I have heard testimonies to this effect and I have also seen these things with my own eyes. I believe that God *can* heal the sick in answer to prayer. I also believe that God not infrequently *does* heal the sick in this way.

But I do *not* believe that God answers *all* the prayers that believers offer up for the healing of the sick. I also do *not* believe that every sick person can be healed in answer to prayer.

There are people who argue that those who cannot be healed through prayer must either be completely lacking in faith or else have insufficient faith. But such an argument is untenable. I believe the reason that many people are not healed in answer to prayer is not that their faith is too small but that their prayer is not according to the will of God. In other words, it may be God's will that their illness should continue until the time fixed for healing arrives or until their time to leave the world arrives. (19)

This is the assurance we have in approaching God: that if we ask anything according to his will, he hears us.

                                        1 John 5:14

When God causes his children to be ill for a prolonged period, it is not always because he wants to discipline them and bring them to the point of abandoning their sin. Sometimes his purpose is to edify them through their illness and enable them to learn deeper lessons than they have learnt hitherto. Consider lessons such as patience, waiting, obedience to God's will, and sympathy – many lessons of this kind must be learned in suffering and cannot be learned without it.

There are times when God causes his children to be tested in the home or to incur losses in business or to suffer physical illness. But it is through these bitter sufferings that God tests and teaches those who love him, so that in the end they become holier, more nearly perfect, more like himself and much more usable in his hands. All this enables them to serve him better and to bring more glory to his name. In the future, when his glory is revealed, they will receive the greater reward. If God has such a marvellous purpose for someone, should he answer the prayers of the sick person and of those who love him when they plead that he will be healed quickly? (19)

Month 4: Day 1   Blessed are the obedient

As Jesus was saying these things, a woman in the crowd called out, 'Blessed is the mother who gave you birth and nursed you.' He replied, 'Blessed rather are those who hear the word of God and obey it.'   **Luke 11:27, 28**

The Lord Jesus tells us with his own lips that those who hear God's word and obey it are more blessed than his mother Mary. We only need to listen carefully to God's word and, after hearing it, to hold it fast and, in dependence on the grace and strength that God bestows on us, do all we can to obey it.

He teaches us to be holy – and we turn away from all unclean and lascivious thoughts and words and deeds. He teaches us to be sincere – and we eschew all lying, craftiness, false pretences and cheating. He teaches us to be humble – and we respect all that is worthy of respect, we obey all that ought to be obeyed and in all things we refrain from self-display.

He teaches us to love other people – and this means that in all our affairs we seek the profit of others and we take account of others; that we consider others as we consider ourselves. He teaches us to be faithful – and this means that we bend every effort to carry out wholeheartedly all the tasks and duties, large and small, that lie before us, neither shrinking from trouble nor yielding to idleness.

We will observe every word in his teaching. In this way he will bless us according to his promise and, through us, will cause other people to be blessed. (12)

Month 4: Day 2   The testimony of transformed lives

A large crowd of Jews found out that Jesus was there and came, not only because of him but also to see Lazarus, whom he had raised from the dead. So the chief priests made plans to kill Lazarus as well, for on account of him many of the Jews were going over to Jesus and putting their faith in him.   **John 12:9–11**

A small number of Christians have special powers of speech, and can preach the gospel of God with great clarity and plainness. But the majority of Christians are not gifted in this way. Yet all Christians can make use of transformed lives to witness silently for the Lord Jesus. I frequently observe saints who, though lacking the gift of speech, influence the lives of many and attract others to the Lord Jesus simply through their transformed lives.

In view of this, believers who lack the gift of speech and cannot testify for the Lord Jesus with their lips in the way that some others can, need not be in the least discouraged or dispirited – under the impression that they themselves can neither work for the Lord nor lead other people to him. It is only necessary that their lives be truly transformed by the Lord's great power and they will become those who bear silent testimony for the Lord. They will be like Lazarus who could cause people, through seeing him, to be greatly influenced and to acknowledge that Jesus is truly the Saviour of mankind. (13)

Month 4: Day 3   The consequences of obedience or disobedience

He went out to meet Asa and said to him, 'Listen to me, Asa and all Judah and Benjamin. The Lord is with you when you are with him. If you seek him, he will be found by you, but if you forsake him, he will forsake you.'

2 Chronicles 15:2

The condition of our being blessed in the sight of God – apart from faith – is obedience. God regards obedience as being of far greater importance than presenting offerings.

Many of the blessings that God bestows are experienced only by those who obey him. Those who obey him, he protects and on them he bestows his favour. He loves those who obey him and also dwells with them. His messenger encamps around them, delivering them and protecting them. Their lives are both joyful and peaceful. So no matter what trials and suffering and attacks and misfortunes come upon them, no one can harm them.

Those who hear the word of God but do not obey it, are in a very different situation. They do not share the blessings that God prepares for those who love him, nor are they joyful and peaceful like those who hear the word of the Lord and obey it. So long as they are free from adversity, they may be able to pass relatively peaceful lives but when trials descend upon them, they are unable to stand. Their life is like the house built on sand: as soon as it is struck by floods, it collapses and the destruction is very great. (16)

I will hasten and not delay to obey your commands.
               Psalm 119:60

This was the attitude of David in the presence of God. As
soon as he received God's commands he hastened to obey
them. He regarded God's affairs as of far greater importance
than his own. In order to obey God's commands, he did not
hesitate to jettison his own convenience and enjoyment. He
recognised that the most important duty in his whole life was
to obey God's commands.

Oughtn't we to adopt the same attitude? As soon as
we have received God's directions, we should on no account
delay but stir ourselves to follow them immediately.

Furthermore we shouldn't stop to calculate whether,
through doing this, we would find ourselves involved in
fatiguing labour. For if we were to pause and go into such
matters, we might allow anxiety to creep in and be tempted
to withdraw, losing the will to obey. In these circumstances,
we would be capable of unearthing many reasons to justify
and acquit ourselves. But probably not one of these would be
the real reason. The real reason would simply be that we
were unwilling to obey – that we dared not obey, and nothing
more. But if we obeyed God's commands without delay,
these dangers would never arise. (16)

He who did not spare his own Son, but gave him up for us all – how will he not also, along with him, graciously give us all things?   **Romans 8:32**

Christ promises his bride that she will dwell with him, that she will be glorified with him, that she will be co-inheritor with him, that she will exercise authority with him and that she will reign with him. The promises are naturally grand beyond compare.

God is bound to carry out what he has promised. He has already provided great and reliable evidence to show how earnest and how fervent is the love with which he loves his bride. This evidence is that he has already first given himself to her and that, in order to save her, he shed his own blood and, in order to redeem her, he laid down his life. He loved her and sought to win her as his bride but without first delivering her from sin and death, it would have been quite impossible to do this.

So, in order to save her, he was willing to be crucified, himself bearing her sin on the tree. It was through his death that she received life. He loved her enough to die for her. Most people would do anything for their own bodies and their own lives. Since Christ gave up his body and his life in order to win the church as his bride, is it likely that he will withhold any good thing from her? (1)

Month 4: Day 6   The conduct of Christ's bride

Dear friends, now we are children of God, and what we will be has not yet been made known. But we know that when he appears, we shall be like him, for we shall see him as he is. Everyone who has this hope in him purifies himself, just as he is pure.   **1 John 3:2, 3**

Christ is holy! If we aspire to be his bride, then we must eschew all impure thoughts, words, deeds and habits and become holy people.

Christ is sincere! If we aspire to be his bride, then we must get rid of deceitful and vain thoughts, words, deeds and habits and become sincere people.

Christ is loving and compassionate! If we aspire to be his bride, then we must do away with all self-seeking, hatred, envy, slander, cursing, quarrelling and violence and become loving and compassionate.

Christ is humble and meek! If we aspire to be his bride, then we must empty ourselves of all pomposity, love of glory, fishing for praise, seeking for fame, pride, self-trust and insulting behaviour and become humble people.

Our bridegroom is Christ. With his penetrating vision and from his stance of absolute justice, he will judge whether we are worthy or not to be his bride. In view of this, we ought always to look away to him and be ever seeking that we shall appear before him without shame. (1)

May God himself, the God of peace, sanctify you through and through. May your whole spirit, soul and body be kept blameless at the coming of our Lord Jesus Christ. The one who calls you is faithful and he will do it.

1 Thessalonians 5:23, 24

We have a tendency to dwell on our weaknesses and as a consequence we tend to become dispirited and to lose heart. This is truly a major mistake. It is right that we should be aware of our weaknesses but, having become aware of them, we must trust the promise of Christ when he assured us of his help: 'My grace is sufficient for you, for my power is made perfect in weakness' (2 Corinthians 12:9).

We may learn from these words not only that our sanctification need suffer no hindrance from our weakness but also that, on the contrary, our weakness may be the opportunity for the power of Christ to be increasingly manifested in us. Our Lord also provided authority over serpents (the devil) and over scorpions (sin); he promised that we would overcome all the power of the enemy, and that nothing would by any means harm us. Since we can be so empowered, is there any limit to what we can do?

The apostle Paul fully believed the doctrine that believers could be sanctified; he also clearly knew the source of believers' sanctification. How greatly the words of 1 Thessalonians 5:23, 24 can comfort and encourage us!

Let us renounce all right to ourselves and offer up our bodies and minds to God! Let us look away to our Lord's great power and might and allow him to do his own work! (1)

Nathan said to David, 'You are the man!' . . . David said to Nathan, 'I have sinned against the Lord.'

2 Samuel 12:7, 13

Whenever God causes us to observe the sins of other people, it is not in order to provide fuel for our anger and criticism; it is not so that we may curse and condemn them; it is in order that we may have a mirror to reflect our own features.

So long as we do not frustrate God's expectation, and so long as we use this 'mirror' for this purpose, we will surely become aware of our own sins from what we observe of other people's sins. We will certainly be unable to repeat what we have done before – that is, get angry with, criticise, anathemise and condemn other people. All that we will be able to do is prostrate ourselves in shame and humility before God and confess our sins to him, saying, 'I have sinned against the Lord!'

If only we could do this, then we would daily move further and further away from sin and nearer and nearer to God; our lives would become holier; we would be more blessed and used by God and more able to sympathise with, forgive and help people.

O God! Whenever I observe someone falling into sin, enable me to hear it if you are saying to me, 'You are the man!' (12)

Month 4: Day 9 — Starting with what we have

'How many loaves do you have?' he asked. 'Go and see!' When they found out, they said, 'Five – and two fish.'

Mark 6:38

Beloved fellow-believers! The Lord repeats the same question today: 'How many loaves do you have?' And when he addresses this question to you, how will you reply? Your natural endowments may not be 100 per cent acute; your speech may not be fluent; your physical frame may not be robust; your home may not be very wealthy; and what you do possess may not be enough of itself to enable many people to eat to the full. But these are not what the Lord Jesus is questioning you about. He only asks, 'How many loaves do you have?'

All that you possess may not amount to very much but you cannot say that you have nothing. It is your brain that enables you to think at this very moment. It is your body that makes you capable of action. It is your mouth that enables you to frame different words. It is your feet that plod along the road. Your strength, your opportunities, your time, your money are available for you to use. If you feel that you have nothing – what about all those things?

'Five loaves and two fish.' The disciples told the Lord in their day what their true situation was. So what about you today? (14)

Month 4: Day 10   Offering what we have to Jesus

'Bring them here to me,' he said.   Matthew 14:18

Beloved fellow-believers! The Lord is asking today for what you have. And he says to you: 'Bring them here to me!' How will you respond?

Give thought to all that the Lord has done for you! For your sake he humbled himself and came into the world; for your sake he became poor and endured all kinds of affliction and adversity; and for your sake he was crucified on the cruel cross. And that was all because of his great love for you.

When you ponder all that he did and all that he endured for you, how can you do other than love him? And if you love him, won't you joyfully offer up to him all that you have? If you know of his great power, if you know that he can do the things you cannot do and use the most insignificant offerings presented by the most insignificant people to accomplish the great work of saving many people – how can you do other than put your trust in him? And if you have confidence in him, won't you offer up to him all that you have without delay?

He will willingly receive all that you offer him; and, just as in biblical times he used the five loaves and two fish so that a crowd of 5,000 men could eat to the full, so in our own day he will use the weak bodies and minds that we offer up to him so that many people may be blessed.

The one who works wonders is the Lord; the one who presents the offerings is you. But unless you first do your part and make the offering, you cannot hope to see the Lord's great power and glory manifested in you. (14)

He directed the people to sit down on the grass. Taking the five loaves and the two fish and looking up to heaven, he gave thanks and broke the loaves. Then he gave them to the disciples, and the disciples gave them to the people.
                                                Matthew 14:19

If you take five loaves and two fish, and do not break them up, they are only sufficient to distribute to seven people at the most. The more you break them up, and the greater the number of fragments into which you break them, the greater the pain (if we may speak in this way) that they experience, but against this is the fact that the number of those who can eventually participate is greatly increased.

The loaves and fish which we offer to the Lord are symbolic of ourselves. Since the Lord wants to use us in providing food for many people to eat to the full, it follows that he must first break us up into fragments. Through the Lord's action, we lose our original fine appearance and our original value and are called upon to suffer considerable pain, which we find uncongenial. Yet it is as a result of our suffering loss and pain, that we can become usable in the hands of the Lord. For it is only then that we can be made available to many people who can thus eat to the full.

Moreover the extent of our usefulness to the Lord is in proportion to the extent of the pain and loss that we suffer when the Lord takes us into his hands to break us up. The greater the number of fragments into which the loaves are broken, the greater the number of those who can eat to the full. The greater the suffering for the Lord that a believer experiences, the greater the number of those who may be blessed through him.

May the Lord break us up into small fragments so that more and more people may be blessed and satisfied through us! (14)

He cuts off every branch in me that bears no fruit, while every branch that does bear fruit he trims clean so that it will be even more fruitful.   **John 15:2**

Christians ought to bear much fruit – both in their words and in their deeds. I have not known a Christian whose manner of life is upright who cannot lead people to the Lord.

We must, however, ask ourselves the question: If our manner of life is *not* pleasing to God, how can we talk of leading people to the Lord? Many Christians today are not bearing fruit and, arguably, this means that the Lord will cut them off. But the Lord at present still tolerates them, hoping that the day will come when they will yet bear fruit.

In the Bible we are also told that when a branch bears fruit he trims it clean. But how does he trim it? It is by taking the knife and the saw and by applying them to the branch. When a branch is trimmed, it naturally suffers. However, these sufferings are good for it.

Sometimes when a believer is involved in suffering, he is tempted to think that the Lord has abandoned him. When zealous believers, particularly, are involved in this kind of suffering, they may not understand why the Lord wants to treat them in this way for, contrary to expectation, they appear to be worse off than their lukewarm brothers and sisters.

But the explanation can be found in our Scripture verse. The branch that bears fruit, he trims clean. So all who bear fruit, the Lord will trim clean. Those who bear much fruit, the Lord will trim even more.

But those who do not bear fruit, the Lord will cut off. (4)

I am the vine; you are the branches. If a man remains in me and I in him, he will bear much fruit; apart from me you can do nothing.   **John 15:5**

How can branches bear much fruit? Without question it is by being united to the trunk. If believers aspire to bear good fruit in word and deed, then they must be joined to the Lord. If a believer can maintain communication with the Lord and be joined to him, then naturally he will be characterised by good deeds, just as branches blossom and bear fruit.

This leads us to another truth. Christ said, 'Apart from me you can do nothing.'

Why is it that people are not joined to the Lord? It is because there is something between them and the Lord which hinders them from being joined to the Lord and takes away their readiness to listen to what the Lord has to say.

The thing that hinders is sin in people's hearts and their unwillingness to confess it. Naturally when a believer finds himself in this situation, he is not only incapable of being joined to the Lord, he is also unwilling to be in contact with him. The major reason for the failure of many believers is the existence of sins that are hidden.

I hope that each one of us will come now into the presence of the Lord and ask him to do away with all that hinders our communication with him so that from now on we may be joined to him. (4)

To godliness, [add] brotherly kindness; and to brotherly kindness, love.   **2 Peter 1:7**

A Christian must first have love for his fellow-Christians, and only then can he have love for all people. We are constantly faced with the spectacle of friction between believer and believer – ill-will, envy, party-spirit and the like. Yet at the same time, these Christians energetically promote the work of evangelism, asserting that they want to lead many people to obtain salvation in Christ. We know, of a certainty, however, that this kind of effort does not spring from love. For if these believers truly had a love for the people, they would long ago have loved one another.

On the other hand, some believers do love their fellow-Christians, but at that point they stop and go no further. It is not that they are incapable of loving everybody but that they have not given thought to everybody. They have not yet realised that it is their duty to love everybody.

Believers who truly love each other still need to go a step further. They must take the love that they have towards each other and learn how to extend it to people in general. They must be concerned about the interests of others.

When once a believer has mastered this particular lesson, then not only is God pleased to choose him, but he himself is certain to be 100 per cent willing to engage in the work of God. (12)

Blessed are you when men hate you, when they exclude you and insult you and reject your name as evil, because of the Son of Man. Rejoice in that day and leap for joy, because great is your reward in heaven. For that is how their fathers treated the prophets.   Luke 6:22, 23

Does the fact that we encounter the hatred of the world make us sad or make us suffer? No! Not merely are we free from sadness or bitterness on this account; on the contrary we are happy and joyful. There are two reasons for this.

First, the hatred of the world is firm evidence that we belong to Christ and that we are loyal to him.

Second, our Lord promises that because we suffer the world's hatred on earth he will bestow on us a great reward in heaven. A precious promise like this brings us joy and hope; it also brings us strength and courage. Never again shall we fear the hatred of the world. Whenever we suffer the hatred of the world we shall refuse to regard this occurrence as our shame or misfortune; rather, we shall regard it as our glory and as a means to blessing.

Our Lord has never spoken lies; He has never taken back his words. As he has spoken, so will he act. What he has promised, he will fulfil. According to his promise, if we are hated, rejected and reviled for his name's sake, we shall in heaven receive a great reward. We ought therefore to trust his words implicitly. (19)

I die every day – I mean that, brothers – just as surely as I glory over you in Christ Jesus our Lord.
                                        1 Corinthians 15:31

This experience of Paul – 'I die every day' – should be the experience of every servant of the Lord; in fact, of every Christian. With a resolve of this nature, Christians would covet nothing in the world and fear nothing in the world.

When Satan places before us such things as prestige, honour, profit and gain, we would say to him, 'Today I die. What would I do with those things?' Similarly when Satan threatens us with suffering, danger, invective and persecution, we would say to him, 'Today I die. Why should I still be afraid of such things?' When Satan uses the prospect of death to terrify us, we would say to him, 'Fine! Couldn't be better! I will today prepare to die!'

There are times when Satan uses the attractive things of the world to tempt us and there are other times when he uses all kinds of hateful things with which to threaten us. If we are attracted by his bait, we shall be caught on his hook. If we are fearful in the face of his threatening, we are in danger of capitulating to him. But so long as we maintain the resolution, 'Today I die,' then all of his devices become ineffective. (19)

Those who were in the boat worshipped him, saying,
'Truly you are the Son of God.'   Matthew 14:33

'"If you can"?' said Jesus. 'Everything is possible for
him who believes.'   Mark 9:23

When we give serious thought to our own little faith, how
ashamed we ought to be! We are perfectly well aware that our
Lord possesses great authority and great power and that he
can subdue all the frightening things that threaten us. But as
soon as we let our eyes wander to our environment, then
doubts and fears begin to arise just as if we had no one at all in
whom to trust or on whom we could rely.

If we genuinely trusted the Lord, not only could we walk,
as it were, on the water, we could also do many things even
greater and more wonderful than this. Now and in the future,
God will still do many wonderful things and manifest his
glory to those who believe in him. With Christ as our saviour
and as our friend, as our guarantor and as our help in all
times of need, what is there for us to fear?

Do not fix your eyes on the violent wind that rages on the
sea, nor look at the turbulent waves beneath your feet. Only
put your trust in the Lord and look away to him. You will
then experience the great and wonderful things that the Lord
will do in you. (19)

The next morning the Jews formed a conspiracy and bound themselves with an oath not to eat or drink until they had killed Paul.   **Acts 23:12**

So long as those who belong to God continue to worship him, do his will and carry out his work faithfully, they need not fear any danger or distress. Without God's permission, no one can harm even a hair of our heads. Even if those wishing to harm a believer were as numerous as those who wished to harm Paul (Acts 23:12–32), it would be necessary for God just to move his fingers slightly and he could bring to nought their plots and resolutions and leave them without trace. For no matter how strong men's resolutions may be, they would not survive even a minute's resistance from God.

The power and influence of evil men appear to be so strong and established that nothing can shake them, whereas they are in fact so brittle that they cannot survive even a single stroke from God. The situation of those who worship God may appear to be hazardous in the extreme, whereas it is as hard and solid as metal.

We should not be fearful that evil men will harm us; what we should fear is failing to worship God rightly or do his work faithfully. We need not fear, even if the forces mustered by Satan were overwhelmingly strong numerically; all we need fear is failing to maintain our walk with God. We ought not to be afraid that forty or so men have made a vow to kill us; our fear should be that we might fail to serve God as courageously and as loyally as Paul did. (9)

They were furious and gnashed their teeth at him. But Stephen, full of the Holy Spirit, looked up to heaven and saw the glory of God, and Jesus standing at the right hand of God. 'Look,' he said, 'I see heaven open and the Son of Man standing at the right hand of God.'

Acts 7:54–56

This is an incident that is well worth our attention. When disciples of Christ courageously bear witness to his name and his gospel, and when, as a consequence, they arouse people's anger and are humiliated, persecuted and treated with violence, then even Christ who is seated at God's right hand will arise from his seat and stand up, thus indicating his respect for them and his welcome to them. What a glorious episode this is!

Let us suppose that we have been given the opportunity to meet some great personality and that when he sees us approaching, while we are still some distance away, he rises from his seat to welcome us. We would regard this mark of respect on his part as an unparalleled honour.

And what of this action of Christ, the Son of God? He has been glorified by God; he has been exalted far above all; he has been given a name which is above every name; and he has been established as King of kings and Lord of lords. This is the one who stands up as a mark of respect for and of welcome to those disciples who have suffered persecution and laid down their lives for his name's sake. Such an honour is infinitely greater than that accorded to us by any earthly potentate. (11)

Whoever can be trusted with very little can also be trusted with much, and whoever is dishonest with very little will also be dishonest with much.   **Luke 16:10**

What can I say for you? With what can I compare you, O Daughter of Jerusalem? To what can I liken you, that I may comfort you, O Virgin Daughter of Zion? Your wound is as deep as the sea. Who can heal you?
                                        Lamentations 2:13

Committing a sin may be compared with making a breach in the wall of a dyke. No matter how small the breach is to begin with, no matter how little it attracts attention, so long as it remains in existence it is capable, sooner or later, of bringing about a major disaster.

May I urge you, then, to pay close attention to any breaches that occur in your life. A little doubt, a little covetousness, a little sexual immorality, a little love of fame, a little envy, a little deceit, a little pride: these breaches are all very small but capable of bringing about major catastrophes.

Maybe you utter a few untruths, a few slanders, a few complaints; maybe you acquire a few possessions dishonestly; maybe you indulge in a few secret evils; maybe you conspire with others to engage in deceit; maybe you wear a false mask; maybe you allow certain bad habits to develop or become careless in your conduct. These too are all small breaches but they can all lead to major calamities.

Once you commit trivial sins you will sooner or later commit major sins. No sin stands alone. You only need to commit one kind of sin and, before long, you will commit a second, then a third and a fourth and a fifth; and who knows where it will all end? (16)

Month 4: Day 21   Who or what is 'spiritual'?

Brothers, I could not address you as spiritual but as worldly – mere infants in Christ. I gave you milk, not solid food, for you were not yet ready for it. Indeed, you are still not ready. You are still worldly. For since there is jealousy and quarrelling among you, are you not worldly? Are you not acting like mere men?

1 Corinthians 3:1–3

On a number of occasions during the past few years I have heard someone described as being a spiritual Christian or a spiritual preacher. I have also heard people referred to as being not spiritual.

Enquiring more closely into what people mean by 'spiritual,' we find that it usually has reference to zeal. The people who make these appraisals seem to think that when a certain individual zealously attends meetings, zealously makes offerings and zealously bears witness, then that individual is a spiritual Christian.

Other people may describe a person as spiritual when his or her beliefs are orthodox.

There are yet others who reserve the description spiritual for those who emphasise speaking in tongues or seeing visions or having dreams or being caught up or falling prostrate on the ground or dancing or crying out. And preachers who do these things are described as spiritual preachers.

But when the Bible uses the word spiritual it does not have reference either to zeal or to orthodoxy of doctrine; still less does it refer to visions, dreams, prostration, dancing and so on. If we want to understand what is the basic meaning of 'spiritual' we must search the Scriptures very carefully. (16)

Are you not acting like mere men?   1 Corinthians 3:3

It is clear from 1 Corinthians 3:1–3 that the apostle Paul divides believers into two classes. One of these classes is carnal, or worldly; these are babes in Christ who can take only milk. The other class is spiritual; these are the ones who can take solid food.

Paul also tells us that being carnal or worldly is to act like mere men. Even though an individual may be very zealous and even though the doctrines he holds may be quite orthodox, if he still acts like a mere man then he is worldly. Even though an individual should speak in tongues every day and constantly see visions, if he acts like a mere man he is still worldly. He may preach the word, be of help to many people and even lead many to believe in the Lord; but if he acts like a mere man he is still worldly.

Paul points to the prevalence of envy, strife and divisions as being manifestations of acting like mere men. To hanker after the commodities and benefits that we see around is to act like mere men. No matter how splendid the projects on which we are engaged, as long as our aim is to attract attention to ourselves and to call forth commendation, we are acting like mere men.

To be mendacious, to utter untruths, to be engaged in deceitful practices, to be insincere in our relationships with other people; to cherish a critical spirit, to stand in judgment of others, to curse and condemn people; to be stubborn, unwilling to listen to exhortation from others, to be self-satisfied; to be void of patience, to be violent in speech, to lack meekness and kindliness in conversation and conduct: all these may also be ways of acting like mere men. (16)

Brothers, if someone is caught in a sin, you who are spiritual should restore him gently . . . If anyone thinks he is something when he is nothing, he deceives himself.   **Galatians 6:1–3**

Who can be reckoned as spiritual? Spiritual Christians are those who do not act like mere men – whether in what they say, in what they do, in the way they treat people or in their work. They consistently act in obedience to the Spirit so that their lives are full of the fruits of the Spirit. According to the teaching of Scripture, these and these only are truly spiritual.

To be correctly described as spiritual, a person must be living a holy life and be obedient to the Holy Spirit. Otherwise, he cannot be described as spiritual, no matter how pure or how orthodox his beliefs are, no matter how abundant his knowledge of the Bible, no matter how many unusual experiences he has had, no matter how much work he has done for the Lord and no matter how many people he has helped and guided.

If Christians truly understand the meaning of spiritual, they will know when they are worldly and not up to standard. From now on, none of us should think of ourselves as being truly spiritual simply because other people call us spiritual. Nor should we class ourselves as spiritual simply on the basis of our own estimation. In order to decide whether or not we ourselves, after all, measure up to the standard, the measure we should apply is God's measure. (16)

Praise the Lord, O my soul, and forget not all his benefits. He forgives all my sins and heals all my diseases; he redeems my life from the pit and crowns me with love and compassion. He satisfies my desires with good things, so that my youth is renewed like the eagle's.   Psalm 103:2—5

How many Christians are there who remember to thank God for his favours? It has not yet come home to many Christians that in the sight of God they are not worthy to receive anything whatever. They seem to be under the impression that they have a privileged position and that they may demand from God blessings of every kind. If God withholds these blessings they regard him as being in debt to them.

Since many Christians do not know what it means to express gratitude to God for his grace as they should, they simply do a little work for God, present some offerings to him and give help to a few people. They then boast of their merits. They display their achievements and look upon themselves as having built up other-worldly merit in the sight of God and as being – as it were – first-class statesmen. But if they were to experience a little suffering or misfortune, they would immediately complain to God and think that he had treated them harshly.

If only these Christians could realise that they are surrounded by the abundant grace of God; and that of all the benefits that they have received there is not one that they are worthy or have a right to receive! With such a realisation of God's grace they would feel ashamed of their foolish thoughts and deeds. (8)

We know that in all things God works for the good of those who love him, who have been called according to his purpose.   **Romans 8:28**

Suffering and grief can easily make the sufferer dispirited and even despairing. But no matter when you encounter suffering or grief, you must on no account become dispirited or despairing. Even less must you doubt or forsake the Lord or lose your faith. It must be fixed in your mind that nothing appointed by the Lord can be wrong. One day, sooner or later, you will understand fully that whatever the Lord does, it is motivated by love. He fashions the affairs that you encounter so that they work out for your good.

True, on many occasions he allows you to suffer minor losses but that is with a view to their eventually bringing you great benefits. He allows you for a limited period to eat a certain amount of bitterness but the end in view is your eternal satisfaction.

Your knowledge is limited and your vision extends only so far. You see only the things that are immediately ahead of you but the distant future is outside your vision. Yet the Lord has a comprehensive plan for you. His treatment of you is not decided by your own knowledge, which is limited; it is determined by his unlimited wisdom and his abounding love.

Therefore no matter what you may meet, you should not allow yourself to be troubled by doubts, nor ought you to begin complaining. All you need to do is to trust the Lord wholeheartedly, to wait for the Lord, to endure adversity and always to remember the words of the Lord: 'You do not realise now what I am doing, but later you will understand' (John 13:7). (19)

Jesus loved Martha and her sister and Lazarus. Yet when he heard that Lazarus was sick, he stayed where he was two more days. Then he said to his disciples, 'Let us go back to Judea.'   **John 11:5–7**

This is a very surprising episode. Since Jesus loved Martha and her sister and Lazarus, you would think that when he heard that Lazarus was sick he would have made his way to the home at Bethany immediately and healed Lazarus of his disease. The Lord, who was full of compassion, had never at any time let people down and caused them to lose hope. Why should it be only on this occasion that he waited until Lazarus had died before setting out for Bethany? The Lord Jesus did not go *before* Lazarus died and then heal him; what Jesus did was to wait until *after* Lazarus had died and then go and raise him from the dead. Why did Jesus act in this way?

I believe there were three reasons. First, in order that the joy of Martha and Mary should abound; second, to strengthen the faith both of the sisters and also of the disciples; and third, so that many Jews would believe in him.

So it was much better to go later rather than earlier. The Lord was not capable of making a mistake. Had he regarded it as better to go earlier, he would undoubtedly have gone earlier. And if he chose to delay, as he did, it was patently for a good purpose. (14)

Jesus loved Martha and her sister and Lazarus. Yet when he heard that Lazarus was sick, he stayed where he was two more days. Then he said to his disciples, 'Let us go back to Judea.'   **John 11:5–7**

There are times when we give ourselves to pray about a certain matter, and we are hopeful that what we pray for will soon be granted. But, contrary to our hopes, a long time passes and the Lord has still not answered our petition. We carefully reconsider what we are praying for and decide that the prayer does not seem unreasonable. We then ask, with some perplexity, 'Has the Lord forgotten us? Can it be that his promises are unreliable?' When these questions force themselves upon us, we cannot avoid feeling weak and dispirited, and we are conscious of hurt. Some reach the point of losing their faith.

But as soon as we ponder this episode of the Lord Jesus raising Lazarus, we are immediately comforted and strengthened. For we now understand that often when the Lord does not immediately carry out what we ask him to, it is not that he has not heard our petitions, it is because his time has not yet come. From our point of view, it would be best if the Lord gave us what we ask for right away. But the Lord knows that it will be for our greater good if he were to give it to us in the future. It is because he loves us that he delays and does not respond immediately. So long as we maintain our trust in the Lord and quietly wait for him, as soon as his time has come he will give us that which far exceeds what we asked for. We are bound to receive joy, comfort and edification greater than any we have known in the past. (14)

The Lord disciplines those whom he loves, and he punishes everyone he accepts as a son.   Hebrews 12:6

Why is it that after falling into sin we experience times when nothing goes smoothly and we are struck by one blow after another? There are two reasons for this.

One reason is that these things are the natural consequences of sin. For example: if we come to dislike certain people, they naturally come to dislike us; when we give rein to our lusts, it is natural for our bodies to become weak and prone to contract disease; when we lose our tempers, we may be unable to eat or sleep properly.

Another reason is that because the Lord loves us, as soon as he sees us fall into sin, he reproves us so that we may repent and so that we may not again fall into that sin. Rebuke of this kind is not to be taken as evidence that God does not love us, for it does, in fact, testify clearly to the fact that God *does* love us.

God's love is not to be compared with the feelings of those who merely dote on others. The Lord loved us from the first not because we were good or lovable. The fact that he loves us now is still not because we are good or lovable. He loves us simply because he is love. And because he is love, he loves us. How great and how marvellous is love like that! (19)

The Lord appeared to us in the past, saying, 'I have loved you with an everlasting love; I have drawn you with loving-kindness.'   **Jeremiah 31:3**

Since the Lord's love is so great and so wonderful, we should thank him, reverence him and love him; present ourselves to him, obey his word and do the things that please him; undertake the work that he has committed to us and serve him with diligence. It may be that someone will ask us why we would want to do these things. Our only appropriate reply is this: 'In view of the fact that we unlovable people have nevertheless been loved with a great and wonderful love, we cannot do other than get rid of our sins, pursue holiness, obey the Lord's commands, witness for the Lord, and love and help people.'

If only we could profoundly comprehend and unceasingly appreciate the Lord's love, what great joy and what satisfaction we should be conscious of in our lives! What amazing progress would be made in our own love and virtue! What splendid results would accrue from all the work that we do out of love for the Lord and for people!

O Lord! Enable me to ponder at all times the love which you have for me. Use your love more and more to inspire and constrain me. (19)

You also must be ready, because the Son of Man will come at an hour when you do not expect him.

                                              Luke 12:40

The illustration of thieves was used both by the Lord himself and also by his apostles in connection with the circumstances of his return (Luke 12:39; 1 Thessalonians 5:1–11; 2 Peter 3:10). It emphasises the fact that the day of Christ's return is not revealed to us and that it will come suddenly.

Since the day cannot be known, there are many people in the world who are confused in their thinking and sunk in a profound sleep. They are unwilling to believe a doctrine that they look upon as utterly visionary and void of all reality. The fact that the day cannot be known, however, means that believers must be prepared for his return and watching daily. They must diligently serve the Lord and, for the Lord's sake, they must also serve men.

It is very beneficial for us that the Lord Jesus never told his disciples the exact day of his return, for only in this situation do we bend every effort to press ahead, refusing to allow our natural laziness to take control. We often hear of believers who either guess or calculate the day when the Lord Jesus will return. This is not a practice that we should follow, for it does not accord with what our Lord taught with his own lips. What he said was this: 'The Son of Man will come at an hour when you do not expect him.' (2)

Praise the Lord, O my soul, and forget not all his benefits. He forgives all my sins and heals all my diseases; he redeems my life from the pit and crowns me with love and compassion. He satisfies my desires with good things, so that my youth is renewed like the eagle's.   **Psalm 103:2–5**

In thinking of the way in which Mephibosheth was favoured by David (2 Samuel 9), I call to mind the favours that have been showered on us by God.

From the time of our forebears right down until the present, we have all without exception enjoyed the grace and favour of God. But at the same time we have offended God, we have been hostile to God, we have even launched attacks on God. By rights we ought long ago to have been disowned by God. Not one of us is worthy to survive in this world that God has created for us; not one of us is worthy to receive all that he provides for us. No matter how severely God may treat us or punish us, we have no grounds for complaint. At the present time, God does not recompense us according to our sins; on the contrary, he pours out his grace and bestows on us all those spiritual blessings that we are unworthy to receive and, indeed, have never had a hope of receiving. The result is that we poor and pitiable sinners have now become extremely rich and greatly honoured in his Son Christ Jesus.

Because of the favour that David showed to Mephibosheth, Mephibosheth was intensely grateful. Seeing that the favour shown to us by God is so many times greater than that shown to Mephibosheth by David, how much more ought our gratitude to be engraved on our hearts and how much more ought we to express it in our lives! (8)

He said to the woman, 'Did God really say, "You must not eat from any tree in the garden"?'   **Genesis 3:1**

Isn't this a device that the devil still uses in order to delude many Christians? He continually pours words of this nature into their ears and into their hearts and creates doubt as to God's existence, doubts as to God's power, doubts as to God's salvation, doubts as to God's warnings and doubts as to God's promises.

Satan does not say outright that these things are false; what he says is that they are not necessarily true. Rather than urging Christians not to believe, he simply creates doubt in their hearts. Once they begin to doubt God's word, he goes a step further and entices them to rebel against God's commands.

Beware of the devil and his devices! Whenever you are conscious of an impulse to doubt God's word, you ought to be aware that Satan's enticement lies behind it and call God to protect you, deliver you and give you the strength to overcome.

Even more important is it that you take a grip of God's words, that you fully believe them and that you allow not the slightest doubt to remain. The best way to smash this device of the devil is to exercise faith. 'Take up the shield of faith, with which you can extinguish all the flaming arrows of the evil one' (Ephesians 6:16). (19)

The devil led him up to a high place and showed him in an instant all the kingdoms of the world. And he said to him, 'I will give you all their authority and splendour, for it has been given to me, and I can give it to anyone I want to. So if you worship me, it will all be yours.' Jesus answered, 'It is written: "Worship the Lord your God and serve him only."' Luke 4:5−8

God has shown us that the way to circumvent the devices of Satan is to love God above all. When a believer loves God with all his heart and all his soul and all his strength and all his mind, then the devices of Satan are utterly without effect. Those who love God are unwilling to forsake God or to revolt against God in order to obtain what the devil offers. Their spiritual eyes see nothing but God. The love they have for God makes them willing, for the sake of God, to renounce all these benefits and not to look upon it as suffering. By simply acting in this way, they smash the devices of the devil.

The foolish Esau, in order to eat some red stew was prepared to sell his birthright. Afterwards, although he bitterly regretted what he had done, he had no means of correcting his great mistake.

On no account let us take the same road and make the same mistake. For by coveting transitory and trivial fame and gain and the pleasures of the world, we may be deceived by Satan and fall into sin, thus losing our heavenly reward. We ought to remember that 'here we do not have an enduring city, but we are looking for the city that is to come' (Hebrews 13:14). (19)

Peter said, 'Ananias, how is it that Satan has so filled your heart that you have lied to the Holy Spirit and have kept for yourself some of the money you received for the land?'   Acts 5:3

Why did Ananias tell a lie in this fashion and seek to deceive God (Acts 5:1–6)? It was because he sought for empty fame and honour, hoping to make the whole church say how zealous he was, and how he loved people.

It was a case of Ananias being tempted by Satan not when he was engaged in doing evil but when he was engaged in doing a *good* thing. Who could have anticipated that Ananias would be tempted and fall into sin in such a context?

Beloved fellow-believers! It is when you are doing good that you should beware of Satan's temptations. It is when you are doing good that you should beware lest he lead you astray. Beware lest he arouse in you an attitude of seeking fame to the point that you transgress and fall.

Whenever you have borne a good testimony for the Lord, whenever you offer up to God your possessions, whenever you are helping other people and whenever you are giving alms – these are the times when you ought to be particularly careful. Do not allow Satan to place in your heart the desire to seek fame and glory. He uses the superficial fame and glory of the world as a bait to get hold of you.

The way for you to smash his devices is to refuse to swallow his bait. Otherwise, just as today you are lamenting Ananias, so in days to come there will be people lamenting you. (19)

Satan rose up against Israel and incited David to take a census of Israel. So David said to Joab and the commanders of the troops, 'Go and count the Israelites from Beersheba to Dan. Then report back to me that I may know how many there are.'   **1 Chronicles 21:1,2**

This command was also evil in the sight of God; so he punished Israel. Then David said to God, 'I have sinned greatly by doing this. Now, I beg you, take away the guilt of your servant. I have done a very foolish thing.'
          1 Chronicles 21:7, 8

When an individual has successfully completed some project or enterprise he is naturally pleased, proud and boastful. He wants to show off his excellence.

The sin of David lay just here. After winning a great victory, he did not return glory to God. He counted the number of Israelites to show how great was the power of his kingdom and how numerous were his troops. It was God who had enabled him to overcome his enemies and his conduct in showing off like this was greatly offensive to God.

Believers who have special abilities and achievements are prone to fall into the sin of pride and boasting, showing off these special abilities and achievements. But this kind of sin is most abhorrent to God. When people sin in this way, they take away glory from God; they overthrow God from his rightful position and occupy it themselves. Transgression of this kind is extremely grave. When a person sins in this way, not only do his special good points lose their value but also he is immediately brought low by God. In the Bible, there are not a few records of this kind of thing happening, including the story referred to above. (19)

Be completely humble and gentle; be patient, bearing with one another in love. Make every effort to keep the unity of the Spirit through the bond of peace.

Ephesians 4:2, 3

Those who in this world genuinely belong to Christ are no more than a little flock. How important it is, then, that the disciples of Christ should be united, that they should help each other and should stand together on one battle line to engage in combat with Satan.

Yet many Christian warriors do not join forces to resist being shamed; on the contrary, they are disunited and they suspect and envy one another. For only a trivial matter a clash of ideas leads to quarrelling. As a consequence the army of the Lord is broken up into separate parts. To hope that in circumstances like these they can overcome the enemy, is like looking for fish on trees.

Satan, who holds the power of the air, fears us operating in harmony. He bends every effort to provoke us into developing bad feelings for each other and into separating from one another. He operates most successfully by attacking us one by one. He first entices us to separate from one another and then to quarrel with one another, even perhaps to the point of being violent to one another. The more fiercely we quarrel, the happier he is as he watches from the air. He stirs us up to become involved in brawling.

Alas! Many believers allow themselves to be caught up in Satan's harmful intrigues and to the end of their lives they never wake up to what is going on. (19)

Jesus immediately said to them: 'Take courage! It is I. Don't be afraid!'   Matthew 14:27

The Lord addresses himself to all those disciples who because of evil or dangerous circumstances become fearful to the point of trembling. He says to them in effect: Do not be afraid! Didn't I say to you that two sparrows are sold for a penny yet not one of them falls to the ground apart from the will of your Father; and that even the very hairs of your head are all numbered? I told you not to be afraid because you are worth more than many sparrows. Do you so easily forget this most precious and reliable promise that I gave you?

I am always watching you; my hands are ever protecting you. Without my permission, what danger can harm even one of the hairs of your head? On one occasion, I spoke only one word, but it was enough to quell the violent wind and cause the fierce waves to be stilled. I could, today, speak one word and cause the dangers you face to be subdued immediately.

My little children! You ought to put your trust in my great power and not be afraid! (19)

Jesus immediately said to them: 'Take courage! It is I. Don't be afraid!'   Matthew 14:27

To all those disciples who are faced with crushing trials and suffering the Lord may also say, in effect: Do not be afraid! Didn't I say to you that if anyone would come after me, he would have to deny himself and take up his cross and follow me? Maybe the trials you face are not light, and the troubles you endure are heavy, but compare them with those that I myself faced and consider which were the harder to endure.

Have you ever been despised and rejected? Have you been acquainted with grief? Have you lived a life of sorrows? Have you ever worn a crown of thorns or a purple robe? Have you had people spit in your face? Has your head been struck with reeds and have you ever been so beaten that your skin was broken and your blood made to flow? And have you, after all that, been nailed to a cross?

I committed no transgression, but, in order to save you, I willingly endured all these things. You were originally the greatest of sinners but, through the bitter suffering I endured, you have attained your present position and happiness.

Aren't you willing to suffer a little hardship through following me? And shouldn't you be much more willing to do so in the light of the fact that I promise to deliver you and protect you in the future?

My little children! You ought to trust me to care for you. Take courage! Don't be afraid! (19)

This is what the Lord says — he who created you, O Jacob, he who formed you, O Israel: 'Fear not, for I have redeemed you; I have called you by name; you are mine. When you pass through the waters, I will be with you; and when you pass through the rivers, they will not sweep over you. When you walk through the fire, you will not be burned; the flames will not set you ablaze.'

Isaiah 43:1, 2

Jesus addresses himself to all disciples who fear and tremble: Don't be afraid! I am your saviour and your close friend; I am your comfort and your strength. I am your help at all times of need.

You are weak but I am strong. You are frequently defeated but I have already won the victory. There are times when you will desert me but I will never desert you. You often forget me but I have never forgotten you. Even if you are faithless to me, I will never be faithless to you.

Unceasingly I prepare for you abundant grace, power, joy and peace. If you are willing to receive them, I will bestow them on you. You may trust in my boundless power to enable you to pass through the fire and not be burned and through the rivers without having them sweep over you; to be in darkness and yet see light. In sorrow you will be comforted. You will be conscious at that time that there is nothing to be feared in all the world.

My little children! You ought to put your trust in my words. Do not be afraid! (19)

Since Christ suffered in his body, arm yourselves also with the same attitude, because he who has suffered in his body is done with sin.   1 Peter 4:1

When Peter saw him, he asked, 'Lord, what about him?' Jesus answered, 'If I want him to remain alive until I return, what is that to you? You must follow me.'
                    John 21:21, 22

Many Christians, especially when confronted by some danger or trial, are curious as to whether their future lot will be congenial or uncongenial, good or bad. This is really a very unhealthy bent of mind. It is not mine to ask what I shall encounter in the future. All I am concerned with is whether *today* I follow the path that I ought to follow or not, whether *today* I do the will of God or not and whether *today* I do the work that I ought to do or not. So, I not only refrain from asking God whether my future circumstances will be favourable or unfavourable, I do not even have the desire to know these things.

If I were shown that my future would be favourable and prosperous, I fear that I should become careless to the point of falling into temptation. On the other hand, if I were shown that I am destined to encounter misfortune and suffering, I fear that I should become anxious and frightened, so leaving an opening for the devil to attack and harm me.

Therefore I have no wish to know what will happen in the future. Instead I arm myself with the attitude of being ready to suffer, so preparing myself to face suffering or anything else that may happen to me. (19)

Month 5: Day 11   Rubbing shoulders with others

As iron sharpens iron, so one man sharpens another.
                                                    Proverbs 27:17

Many people are dissatisfied with the people around them. In their thinking, people anywhere else in the world would be easier to deal with than the people around them.

They do not realise that the most difficult people to deal with in the whole world are not other people but themselves. God places people around them who are not congenial so that they can rub off each other's corners and make them smooth. They will thus become smooth stones in God's bag. God causes us to come into contact with many people who are difficult to live with simply in order that, through them, he can make us smooth.

If the corners remain, we shall then be unable to get on with anyone. In that case, though other people may not inflict suffering on us, we shall certainly inflict suffering on them; and those who are made to suffer by us will not endure that suffering willingly; they will stir themselves to resist us and it will then be impossible to avoid friction and division.

But if, by the grace of God, we humbly and patiently learn to live with the people around us, we shall be equipped to get on well with anyone. (16)

So when the Midianite merchants came by, his brothers pulled Joseph up out of the cistern and sold him for twenty shekels of silver to the Ishmaelites, who took him to Egypt.   **Genesis 37:28**

When his master heard the story his wife told him, saying, 'This is how your slave treated me,' he burned with anger. Joseph's master took him and put him in prison, the place where the king's prisoners were confined.   **Genesis 39:19, 20**

Joseph was sold by his brothers into Egypt as a slave. Afterwards he was falsely accused by the adulterous and shameless wife of his master, as a result of which he was thrown into jail. All these things were according to the will of God. Had God not permitted it, not one of these things would have happened to him.

God wanted Joseph to do a great work and therefore, first of all, he had to take thoroughgoing measures to edify, discipline and train him and thus endow him with the necessary qualifications for doing great things.

God is aware that those who are to accomplish great things for him must learn many lessons – humility, sincerity, loyalty, diligence, patience, willingness to eat bitterness, faithfulness in small things and readiness to bear both responsibility and blame.

Even more is God aware that these lessons cannot be learned in easygoing circumstances. He thus uses the treatment that Joseph received from his brothers, resulting in his being sold into the house of Potiphar, to teach the young man many lessons that he had not had an opportunity to learn earlier. God saw that even these lessons were not enough, so he used the hands of wicked men to send Joseph to jail.

Every step that Joseph took was more bitter but through these he became qualified to accomplish great things. (19)

Month 5: Day 13 — God knows what he's doing!

Pharaoh sent for Joseph, and he was quickly brought from the dungeon. When he had shaved and changed his clothes, he came before Pharaoh. Genesis 41:14

He knows the way that I take; when he has tested me, I shall come forth as gold. Job 23:10

What precious teaching is afforded us by Joseph's imprisonment and release!

We are shortsighted. We are concerned only about the comforts and the joys that lie immediately before us. We do not allow our minds to dwell on the greater benefits that may follow afterwards. Therefore we invariably choose the roads that are flat and smooth and easy to travel.

Yet because God loves us, he constantly treats us not according to our own ideas; he places us in circumstances of suffering and adversity. The purpose of this, on the one hand, is to purge away our dross and to eliminate all impurity and on the other hand, is to teach us many valuable and important lessons.

When we encounter such circumstances, we are totally unwilling to endure them and unprepared to await God's time. We commission people to deliver us; trusting to our own wisdom, we make our own plans and arrangements. But perhaps a month passes, then another; a year, then another — and our hopes have not materialised. Our hearts become impatient in the extreme, and complaints flow like a stream from our lips.

And yet, were they not for our good, God would long ago have delivered us from all these adversities. (19)

The chief cupbearer ... did not remember Joseph; he forgot him.   **Genesis 40:23**

He knows the way that I take; when he has tested me, I shall come forth as gold.   **Job 23:10**

God has never forgotten his children. Were it not in our interest, he would on no account permit any kind of distress or suffering to come upon us. If he ever leads us through circumstances that are hard to bear, we may be sure that he has a high purpose to carry out.

As soon as we have mastered the lessons that he wants us to learn, we need not think up for ourselves a method of escape for he himself will stretch out his hand to deliver us from all misery and adversity. But until his time comes, even if we ourselves devise a method of escape or else plead with someone else to deliver us, we will still be unable to profit from all this; rather, we will be even more conscious of disappointment and have to endure even more bitter suffering.

The best thing for us to do when in circumstances of distress and suffering, is to put our trust in God, wait for him and joyfully endure whatever comes upon us. In such a situation we may learn all kinds of lessons that we would never learn in more congenial circumstances: humility, patience, meekness, goodness, diligence, loyalty, forgiveness, and sympathy.

If we can only endure testing and suffering as Joseph did, we shall certainly be blessed and used as Joseph was. (19)

He took his staff in his hand, chose five smooth stones from the stream, put them in the pouch of his shepherd's bag and, with his sling in his hand, approached the Philistine . . . Reaching into his bag and taking out a stone, he slung it and struck the Philistine on the forehead. The stone sank into his forehead, and he fell face down on the ground.   1 Samuel 17:40, 49

What a truly strange thing! So much was achieved by one small stone! It served to effect deliverance for all the people of Israel.

If God intervenes to bring deliverance, just one small stone can strike and kill a warrior from whom everyone has fled away. And if God himself effects salvation, he can use an extremely weak and insignificant believer to accomplish a work that otherwise could not be accomplished even by thousands of people.

There is a general impression that a powerful enemy can be overcome only by the use of such things as spears and swords. But God used small stones which most people ignore to put the warrior Goliath to death. People normally have the impression that only those who have learning or ability or social position or wealth can accomplish anything great. But God uses believers who are simple, weak, poor and lowly to accomplish wonderful things for him. 'God chose the foolish things of the world to shame the wise; God chose the weak things of the world to shame the strong. He chose the lowly things of the world and the despised things – to nullify the things that are, so that no one may boast before him' (1 Corinthians 1:27–29). (19)

He chose . . . five smooth stones.　　　　**1 Samuel 17:40**

The stone that God used in the hand of David was a smooth stone. For stones to become smooth enough to be made use of, many years of colliding with each other and rubbing each other are necessary.

Those people whom God chooses and uses are also prepared in this way. At the time they are saved, their sins of the past are forgiven but their corners remain.

What are these corners? They are such things as self-pleasing, pride, avarice, envy and temper. Unless these corners are subjected to a very long process of rubbing, they will not be worn down.

In our homes, places of business or wherever, God puts us together with people who are difficult to live with and hard to get along with in order that, through their colliding with us and being rubbed together with us, he can do away with our corners. All that we have to do is to cherish an attitude of thankfulness and obedience and endure this prolonged period of friction. The rubbing continues until we are made smooth. Once that is achieved, our usefulness to God is very great indeed. (19)

Because the Lord had closed her womb, her rival kept provoking her, in order to irritate her . . . In bitterness of soul Hannah wept much and prayed to the Lord.
                                      1 Samuel 1:6, 10

How precious is the teaching in this episode of Hannah (1 Samuel 1)! No matter where we are, no matter whose insults, ridicule, ill-treatment, or attacks we suffer from, we should never offer resistance. We should simply enter quietly into the presence of God as Hannah did; we read that she 'prayed to the Lord.'

When we are subject to insults it may be that we cannot avoid being like Hannah in another respect: she 'wept and would not eat.' God does not reprove us for our weeping, for he knows our weakness. If we go into his presence and give ourselves to weeping and tell him of our bitterness of soul, calling on him to deliver us, he will not only show his sympathy towards us but also wipe away our tears, replacing our bitterness with blessing.

On the other hand, if we are unwilling to endure insults and set out to resist them, we can only make the situation worse; and, as well as dishonouring the name of God and harming other people, we ourselves will suffer even more bitterness. (12)

Early the next morning they arose and worshipped before the Lord and then went back to their home at Ramah. Elkanah lay with Hannah his wife, and the Lord remembered her. So in the course of time Hannah conceived and gave birth to a son. She named him Samuel, saying, 'Because I asked the Lord for him.'
                                        1 Samuel 1:19, 20

The joy that Hannah eventually experienced was a consequence of her having been insulted by Peninnah. Had she not been insulted by Peninnah, she wouldn't have approached God and called on him as she did; still less would she have received the joy and blessing that came later. Peninnah's idea was to ill-treat Hannah but it was as a consequence of her ridicule that Hannah became heir to immeasurable blessing. Presumably, when Peninnah eventually observed the blessing that came to Hannah through calamity, she was vexed with herself for trying to be clever yet failing. She aimed to inflict harm on another person but, on the contrary, she was the means of blessing being brought to her.

Many believers today have experiences similar to those of Hannah. As a consequence of being ridiculed, ill-treated and oppressed, they come to God and make their appeal to him. The result is that they enjoy special blessings. Moreover God often uses ridicule, ill-treatment and oppression to put pressure on his children to draw near to him and to receive from him grace more abundant. God's ways are truly wonderful. With what kindness he treats his children! 'In all things God works for the good of those who love him.' (Romans 8:28). There is no doubt about this whatsoever! (12)

He said to me, 'My grace is sufficient for you, for my power is made perfect in weakness.' Therefore I will boast all the more gladly about my weaknesses, so that Christ's power may rest on me.   **2 Corinthians 12:9**

The apostle Paul suffered from a thorn in the flesh (2 Corinthians 12:7).

Have you any suffering or weakness that may be compared with that thorn? Have you asked the Lord many times to take it away yet never had your wish? Do not be discouraged! If the Lord does not remove this physical weakness of yours, it is in order to manifest his strength even more. Do not forget his words, 'My grace is sufficient for you, for my power is made perfect in weakness.'

Are you in a situation characterised by suffering and testing from which, for a long time now, you have failed to extricate yourselves? Do not be dispirited! Remember that the Lord wants to refine those who belong to him in the same way that gold and silver are refined (Malachi 3:1–3). When gold and silver are smelted it is necessary not only for them to pass through the fire but also to remain in the fire for a long time. The longer they are in the fire, the purer they will be. The fact that God allows you to remain in a situation of testing for a prolonged period is also solely that he may completely get rid of the dross and make you as gold that is refined in the fire. (19)

One night the Lord spoke to Paul in a vision: 'Do not be afraid; keep on speaking, do not be silent. For I am with you, and no one is going to attack and harm you, because I have many people in this city.'   **Acts 18:9, 10**

It has been the experience of some who have been faithful in the work of God and battled for the truth, to be hemmed in, threatened, attacked and persecuted by evil men. Are you among them? And have you, as a consequence, been tempted to lose hope? If so, I urge you: Do not be discouraged!

The apostle Paul was once in this situation. But the Lord said to Paul in a vision: 'Do not be afraid; keep on speaking, do not be silent. For I am with you, and no one is going to attack and harm you, because I have many people in this city.'

That promise was given to Paul of old: it is given to you today. The one who protected Paul will also protect you. It may be that you were commissioned by God to work among a certain people but that you have discovered they are absolutely stubborn and unwilling to receive the message that you are proclaiming to them. If so, you may have reached the point at which you are beginning to lose hope. In that case, I urge you: Do not be discouraged!

There was a prophet of old time who encountered circumstances of this kind. But God said to him, 'I will make you as unyielding and hardened as they are. I will make your forehead like the hardest stone, harder than flint. Do not be afraid of them or terrified by them, though they are a rebellious house' (Ezekiel 3:8, 9). (19)

Jesus told his disciples a parable to show them that they should always pray and not give up.   Luke 18:1

His master replied, 'Well done, good and faithful servant! You have been faithful with a few things; I will put you in charge of many things. Come and share your master's happiness!'   Matthew 25:21, 23

Maybe you have been praying fervently about some matter for a long time, fully convinced that this is in accordance with the will of God, but still haven't received what you have been praying for.

Do not on this account be discouraged! Recall what the Lord Jesus said of the friend who asked for loaves in the middle of the night (Luke 11:5–13) and also the parable of the widow who petitioned the unrighteous judge to obtain justice for her (Luke 18:1–8). Since our Father greatly loves us, he will be all the more ready to hear our petition and to do for us what we have sought for so long.

Maybe you have noticed that other Christians have numerous gifts and splendid opportunities and that their work for the Lord is wide-reaching. You yourself, however, have never enjoyed so many gifts, never encountered such splendid opportunities nor been able to accomplish anything great for the Lord.

Do not be discouraged! What the Lord requires of you is not some great work; what He requires of you is faithfulness. The one who received two talents and gained two more talents is rewarded in exactly the same way as the one who received five talents and gained five more talents (Matthew 25:14–30). (19)

Dear friends, do not be surprised at the painful trial you are suffering, as though something strange were happening to you. But rejoice that you participate in the sufferings of Christ, so that you may be overjoyed when his glory is revealed.   **1 Peter 4:12, 13**

I urge you, my fellow-believers, to take a new look at church history. Consider the Christians of old! On account of confessing the Lord's name and tenaciously holding the faith, many were willing to be imprisoned, to be crucified, to be burnt to death or to be thrown into the arena where they were devoured by wild beasts.

How was it that they could be so courageous, so unwavering, so prepared to suffer? And how could they regard death as going home?

One fundamental reason was that the church at that time had not departed from the teaching of the apostles and had not yet become mixed up with the world.

They believed implicitly the promises of the Lord Jesus; they had the same viewpoint as the Lord. They were perfectly aware that on the reverse side of suffering for the Lord was victory; that on the reverse side of the shame they suffered for the Lord was glory; and that after they had laid down their lives for the Lord, there awaited for them a glorious resurrection. Because their eyes were opened to see what the Lord saw, they could be like the Lord in facing suffering, shame or even death without the slightest fear or hesitation. (11)

The Lord said to Moses and Aaron: 'How long will this wicked community grumble against me? I have heard the complaints of these grumbling Israelites. So tell them, "As surely as I live, declares the Lord, I will do to you the very things I heard you say."'

Numbers 14:26–28

The people grew impatient on the way; they spoke against God and against Moses . . . Then the Lord sent venomous snakes among them; they bit the people and many Israelites died.   Numbers 21:4–6

When the ancient Israelites grumbled against God in the wilderness, they suffered the most terrible retribution. The apostle Paul referred to this episode as a warning to the church. He wrote: 'Do not grumble, as some of them did – and were killed by the destroying angel' (1 Corinthians 10:10). The habit of grumbling is not only evidence that we are dissatisfied with what God is doing, it is also evidence that our attitude to God is one of hostility and rebellion.

The road along which God originally led us is entirely for our good. All that he appoints for us derives from his purposes of love and compassion. Of course, considering the things that he allows us to encounter, there are manifestly times when we cannot escape feeling a measure of pain. But in the end these things lead to our greatest good and happiness.

If we give ourselves to grumbling on account of a little passing suffering, that is surely a case of repaying kindness with injury. When people show us kindnesses, we certainly ought not to repay them with evil. How much more is this the case in regard to God who has dealt with us so abundantly in grace! To bear a grudge against our fellow men and women is sin; how much greater is the sin when we bear a grudge against God! (18)

I am already being poured out like a drink offering, and the time has come for my departure. I have fought the good fight, I have finished the race, I have kept the faith. Now there is in store for me the crown of righteousness, which the Lord, the righteous Judge, will award to me on that day — and not only to me, but also to all who have longed for his appearing.   **2 Timothy 4:6–8**

All true believers are anxious to obey God. But if through obeying God they have to experience suffering, they then hesitate to press on further. Most believers would like to tread the path of obedience to God without incurring suffering but this, in fact, is impossible. The reason is that the path of obedience is a spiritual battlefield and a battlefield is a place of considerable suffering and danger.

Please take note of the expressions that Paul here uses: 'fought the good fight' and 'finished the race.' These two concepts cannot be separated. To tread the path of obedience is to fight the spiritual fight. So long as we are obedient to God, we shall be in conflict with the devil. Because of this, we inevitably encounter hardship when we tread the path of obedience. But it is from these hardships that we go on to learn greater and more jubilant obedience.

We are enabled through hardship to make constant progress and every step of obedience brings another occasion of victory. The more we are willing to obey, the greater the hardship we face. But, so long as we do not retreat or lose heart, the more hardship we suffer, the greater is our progress in the spiritual life. At the same time, the more victories we win, the closer we get to the glory that the Lord has promised us. (16)

When the soldiers crucified Jesus, they took his clothes, dividing them into four shares, one for each of them, with the undergarment remaining. This garment was seamless, woven in one piece from top to bottom. 'Let's not tear it,' they said to one another. 'Let's decide by lot who will get it.' This happened that the Scripture might be fulfilled which said, 'They divided my garments among them and cast lots for my clothing.' So this is what the soldiers did.   **John 19:23, 24**

For you know the grace of our Lord Jesus Christ, that though he was rich, yet for your sakes he became poor, so that you through his poverty might become rich.

2 Corinthians 8:9

We Christians today have position, happiness, blessings, joy and peace. But this is entirely due to the suffering and poverty that the Lord endured for us. In the light of that, can we still live for ourselves? Can we seek for money and fame all our days and not work for the Lord and for our fellow men and women? Having fallen heir to the Lord's abundant love and grace, we cannot, if we are still selfish and self-seeking like other people, be worthy of the Lord who endured such poverty and suffering for us.

There may be times when we are ridiculed and humiliated, when we suffer poverty and hardship. At times like these, we should recall how our Lord's garments were divided among the soldiers and that will be a source of great comfort to us. No matter how much shame we suffer, can it ever be greater than that which was borne by the Lord?

If we constantly meditate on all that the Lord endured for us on Calvary, we will not only be comforted and filled with gratitude, but we will also regard it as a cause for rejoicing when we are called upon to endure what is only trivial and transient suffering for the Lord. (19)

The apostles left the Sanhedrin, rejoicing because they had been counted worthy of suffering disgrace for the Name.   **Acts 5:41**

Thanks be to God! he gave this special kind of grace and glory not only to the early apostles, but also gives it to us today.

Although we may not have been beaten for the name of Christ as the apostles were, yet in different ways we may have suffered for the name. We may have suffered derision, ridicule, insults and invective.

There are some believers who become upset and angry when they are treated in this way; there are those who grieve over it and become heart-broken; and there are others who become fearful and shrink back, no longer daring to confess the Lord's name.

What believers like this need to understand more than anything, is that what they encounter is not to be regarded as misfortune but as blessing, not as shame but as glory. For although we are not worthy to suffer disgrace for the name of Jesus Christ, yet God causes us, like the early apostles, to be 'counted worthy of suffering disgrace for the name.' Once we comprehend that our afflictions are a special kind of grace and a special kind of glory, we will not be upset and angry or grieved and heart-broken; and we will not be fearful and shrink back. Rather, we will be like the early apostles who, after being beaten for the name of the Lord, were able to leave the Sanhedrin rejoicing. (19)

Do you not know that the saints will judge the world?
                                        1 Corinthians 6:2

In the world today we see and hear everywhere things that
cause us unease. We certainly feel at times that we cannot
endure them. As a consequence we want to stir ourselves and
intervene.

If we are faithful disciples of the Lord Jesus, the day will
come when the Lord will exercise judgment on this evil world
and at that time he will endow us with great authority to
exercise judgment with him and set right all the world's
injustices. However, *today* we must start getting rid of all
forms of unrighteousness and sin, and exerting all our
strength to seek holiness and perfection. We must in all our
ways reflect the pattern of the Lord Jesus, follow in his
footsteps, and carry out faithfully all the duties that he
commits to us. Otherwise, not only shall we be unworthy to
serve as future judges, but also our Lord will not dare to
commit to us responsibility of this kind.

Bearing all this in mind, we ought to press strongly ahead
in dependence on the Lord; we ought to turn our backs on all
sin and obey the Lord's commands; and we ought to carry
out wholeheartedly all the duties – large and small – that lie
ahead of us, so that we do not disappoint the Lord by failing
in our appointed tasks. (17)

David stayed in the desert strongholds and in the hills of the Desert of Ziph. Day after day Saul searched for him, but God did not give David into his hands.

1 Samuel 23:14

The Lord is my light and my salvation – whom shall I fear? The Lord is the stronghold of my life – of whom shall I be afraid? When evil men advance against me to devour my flesh, when my enemies and my foes attack me, they will stumble and fall. Though an army besiege me, my heart will not fear; though war break out against me, even then will I be confident.   **Psalm 27:1–3**

Saul occupied the throne and he exercised great authority. He was bent on inflicting harm on David who had neither position nor authority. It was only necessary for Saul to issue a command and David could immediately be arrested.

Yet when we read the biblical records, we find that although Saul concentrated all his powers, mental and physical, in an effort to inflict harm on David, he was never at any time successful. No matter how authoritative Saul's position was, it could never be more authoritative than God's. So long as 'God did not give David into his hands,' there was nothing whatever that Saul could do about it. David's safety was never in the hands of Saul; it was always in the hands of God.

Just as God wielded final authority in days of old, so does he wield final authority today. Just as he was to be relied on in days of old, so is he to be relied on today. No matter how dangerous is the situation in which we are placed or how many secret plots the enemy devises against us, so long as God does not deliver us into his hands, we are perfectly safe. Even though it is a terrifying road along which we travel, it is still the safest road. So although we encounter the violent attacks of evil men, we may do so without suffering loss. (19)

David was greatly distressed because the men were talking of stoning him; each one was bitter in spirit because of his sons and daughters. But David found strength in the Lord his God.   1 Samuel 30:6

So long as we are in the world, none of us who belong to God can escape adversity. This applies in particular to those who are specially used by God. The more grace a believer experiences and the weightier the commission he receives from God, the more numerous are the occasions of adversity that he encounters. For Satan is afraid whenever he observes believers receive more of God's grace; he is even more afraid when believers are specially used by God. So whenever he sees believers receiving more of God's grace or being more and more used by God, the more he threatens them and attacks them. Nor will he desist from attacking them until they are dispirited and begin to stumble.

On the surface, it was Saul and the commanders of the Philistines who troubled and persecuted David, whereas in reality these people were all in the hands of Satan and manipulated by him. Satan perceived that God was pleased with David and using him, so he repeatedly mounted attacks against him. Had David at that time weakened and stumbled, that would have been a major success for Satan.

It seems never to have occurred to Satan that David, during those crises of life and death, consistently 'found strength in the Lord his God.' It was only after the defeat of Satan's final fierce onslaught that for David it became a case of 'after the bitter comes the sweet.' (19)

Month 5: Day 30   Thankful in all circumstances

Though the fig-tree does not bud and there are no grapes on the vines, though the olive crop fails and the fields produce no food, though there are no sheep in the pen and no cattle in the stalls, yet I will rejoice in the Lord, I will be joyful in God my Saviour. The Sovereign Lord is my strength; he makes my feet like the feet of a deer, he enables me to go on the heights.   Habakkuk 3:17–19

The times in our lives that are marked by adversity provide the opportunities for us believers to learn to trust in God. Therefore we should refuse to be despondent; on the contrary, we should rejoice and be glad, giving thanks for God's grace at a time of adversity as much as at any other time.

Thanks be to God – he has saved us and called us. Thanks be to God – he enables us to survive even in adversity. Thanks be to God – he bestows upon us heavenly and spiritual blessings.

Thanks be to God – we have grounds for hope and trust. Thanks be to God – he has endowed us with comfort and gladness. Thanks be to God – he gives us strength to endure tribulation.

Thanks be to God – he has not rewarded us according to our iniquities. Thanks be to God – he has promised us an eternal home in heaven, and a kingdom that can never be moved. Thanks be to God for his glory – eternal and incomparable.

Thanks be to God – he enables us, through trusting the Lord Jesus, to enter into his presence 'with confidence, so that we may receive mercy, and find grace to help us in our time of need' (Hebrews 4:16). (19)

[Moses] saw an Egyptian beating a Hebrew, one of his own people. Glancing this way and that and seeing no one, he killed the Egyptian and hid him in the sand.

Exodus 2:11, 12

There was one occasion in the life of Moses when he failed to wait for God and as a consequence he brought upon himself considerable misfortune and even ran the risk of forfeiting his life (Exodus 2:1–15). It was through him that God had already decided to deliver the people of Israel. But Moses had a hasty temperament and did not wait for God's time to come. As soon as he saw one of his people being oppressed by the Egyptians, he could not suppress his anger and, trusting to his own fleshly courage, put the Egyptian to death and buried him in the sand.

Isn't it a fact that we also often do stupid things like that? As soon as we are insulted and ill-treated, we are filled with indignation and resentment and inclined to repay evil with evil. Or maybe we observe that the evil devices of other people have brought success, so we become restive and the thought is implanted in our hearts that we ourselves should adopt evil ways.

If only we could be patient for a while and wait for God's time to come, he would then, without any fuss, set all injustice to right, just as he attacked Pharaoh and led the whole people of Israel out of Egypt. He observes our weakness and stupidity and therefore makes a point of teaching us. He says: Do not say, 'I'll pay you back for this wrong!' Wait for me and I will deliver you. (9)

The Lord longs to be gracious to you; he rises to show you compassion. For the Lord is a God of justice. Blessed are all who wait for him!　　　　Isaiah 30:18

We need to learn to wait for God in both big things and little things in our daily lives. This is not to say that we should be idle all the time and that we should not apply ourselves to anything; nor is it to say that we should renounce our duties. What it does mean is that we should on no account do anything outside the will of God.

When you are confronted by misfortune or danger, do not be in the least flurried or fearful. Do nothing that God does not permit. Do not put your trust in people who do not belong to God. When you observe evil men engaging in violence, do not allow yourself to be upset to the point of doing evil yourself. Do not repay evil with evil. Do not use methods with which God is not pleased in order to pursue honour, profit or success; do not use your own fleshly methods to help in anything that God is doing.

Waiting for God and living in idleness are totally distinct activities. An idle person is one who is unwilling to carry out the duties and tasks that lie ahead of him; a person who waits for God is one who does nothing that lies outside God's will but who, while waiting, is diligent, every day and every hour, in doing the things that he should, as he follows the path ordained by God. (9)

Let us acknowledge the Lord; let us press on to acknowledge him. As surely as the sun rises, he will appear; he will come to us like the winter rains, like the spring rains that water the earth.   Hosea 6:3

There is one discipline that is closely bound up with the practice of waiting for God. It is to put one's trust in God.

Only those who trust God are in a position to wait for him. The reason that we dare to wait for God is that we trust him. We believe that he will on no account fail us; that he can do the things that we ourselves cannot do; that he is more reliable than anyone in the world; that he will in no circumstances forget us; that he does all things well; that his eyes are watching all who are looking to him and that he hears our petitions.

The more we trust him, the more we dare to wait for him. The extent of our trust in God and the extent of our knowledge of God, are in direct proportion to each other. And only as we know God more, can we trust him more. No wonder the prophet Hosea directed the Israelites to press on to know God! (9)

Month 6: Day 4   The blessings of waiting

Wait for the Lord; be strong and take heart and wait for the Lord.   **Psalm 7:14**

Those who are able to wait for God are truly blessed. In the sight of other people, they may seem to be holding up progress, whereas what they achieve is far in excess of what other people achieve. In the sight of other people, they may seem to be weak and powerless, whereas they are stronger than any other people. Of a certainty they will 'renew their strength. They will soar on wings like eagles; they will run and not grow weary; they will walk and not be faint' (Isaiah 40:31).

They do not lightly undertake any task but once they do so, they will certainly make a success of it. They possess the wisdom and power that comes from heaven, so they can do things that other people cannot do.

Their situation may appear to be very hazardous, whereas it is extremely safe. The path they are treading may appear to be very rough whereas, in point of fact, it is smooth. No one is stronger or more established than those who wait for God. No one is more joyous or more blessed than those who wait for God.

Learning to wait for God is an extremely difficult and an extremely complicated lesson but, once mastered, far more useful than many other lessons. (9)

King Herod arrested some who belonged to the church, intending to persecute them. He had James, the brother of John, put to death with the sword.   Acts 12:1, 2

The apostle James was put to death by Herod. Peter was also arrested by Herod and thrown into prison but in his case God sent an angel in the night to deliver him from the terrible hand of Herod and to bring him out of prison (Acts 12:1–19). Was it only Peter whom God was able to save? Couldn't he also have delivered James? Was God being partial?

God was not being partial. He saw that James' work on earth had been completed and he chose to use the hand of Herod to bring him to glory. But God still had considerable work to commit to Peter so God sent an angel to deliver him.

James was put to death not because he was more unfortunate than Peter; and Peter's deliverance from prison is not to be regarded as evidence that God treated Peter better than he treated James. God's commission to these two men and his appointments for them differed the one from the other so their circumstances naturally differed too.

As far as we ourselves are concerned, we need not enquire as to how God will treat us. If he wants me to be a James, I will praise him. If he wants me to be a Peter, I will also praise him. We have no right to choose for ourselves either the one or the other and no right to ask God what our circumstances will be in the future. (19)

See that no one is sexually immoral, or is godless like Esau, who for a single meal sold his inheritance rights as the oldest son. Afterwards, as you know, when he wanted to inherit this blessing, he was rejected. He could bring about no change of mind, though he sought the blessing with tears.   Hebrews 12:16, 17

The disciples of Christ are of all people those with the greatest future.

   Many Christians concentrate all their thoughts on the few tens of years lying immediately before them and ignore the interests of eternity. They are like the foolish Esau of old who sold his inheritance rights as the eldest son in order to enjoy a single meal. Although he later repented he could not recover from his big mistake.

   We are certainly not people who have no future. We have in fact the greatest, the most splendid and the most illustrious future possible. Our future is not limited to a few tens of years; it is a future that extends to eternity. In order to follow Christ, we are willing to sacrifice a future that lasts only a few years and then is cut short. Nothing is enough to bind our hearts. There is nothing on earth that we covet; there is nothing on earth that we fear.

   Only by holding fast this determination and maintaining this attitude, can we overcome all the seductions of Satan; only thus can we live a life of victory. (19)

Do not worry about your life, what you will eat or drink; or about your body, what you will wear. Is not life more important than food, and the body more important than clothes?   **Matthew 6:25**

We have God as our heavenly Father. The whole world was created by him and all is governed by him. He uttered the words, 'Let there be!' and there was. 'The eyes of all look to you, and you give them their food at the proper time. You open your hand and satisfy the desires of every living thing' (Psalm 145:15, 16). 'He covers the sky with clouds; he supplies the earth with rain and makes grass grow on the hills. He provides food for the cattle and for the young ravens when they call' (Psalm 147:8, 9). 'Every animal of the forest is mine, and the cattle on a thousand hills' (Psalm 50:10).

We are aware that since God has all authority and all power, he can supply for us all that we need; since he is faithful, he is bound to do so; since he greatly loves us, he rejoices to do so.

That being so, we need never again be anxious; we need never ask the question: 'What shall we eat?' or, 'What shall we drink?' or, 'What shall we wear?' If we do become anxious, it shows that we are not trusting him. And that means, in turn, that we are dishonouring him. Does anyone dare to be as impertinent as this? (11)

Jesus said to them, 'Come and have breakfast.' None of the disciples dared ask him, 'Who are you?' They knew it was the Lord.   **John 21:12**

Is it possible that the Lord, who has overcome Satan, broken down the gate of death and assumed authority in heaven and earth, can consistently pay attention to the trivial question of what his disciples have to eat? The answer is, he can.

In any matter that concerns the wellbeing of his disciples, nothing is too big and nothing is too small for him to handle. His authority is so great that he can perform the things that are beyond the power of man; at the same time, his love is so great that he is prepared to do the things that men regard as trivial.

The Lord is as concerned today about those who believe in him and love him as he was in days of old. In the times of our greatest need, he has never failed to come to our aid. There are times when we are confronted by situations that are truly frightening; when we reach the point at which our resources are exhausted; when we are at a loss as to how we can press ahead. At times like these, our Lord, who is so compassionate and loving, will manifest his mighty hand and wonderfully prepare for us the things that we need, just as he did by the Sea of Tiberias. 'Jesus Christ is the same yesterday and today and for ever' (Hebrews 13:8) – what a truthful declaration! (19)

'I'm going out to fish,' Simon Peter told them, and they said, 'We'll go with you.' So they went out and got into a boat, but that night they caught nothing. Early in the morning, Jesus stood on the shore, but the disciples did not realise that it was Jesus.   **John 21:3, 4**

Lazy hands make a man poor, but diligent hands bring wealth.   **Proverbs 10:4**

Only after the disciples had laboured all night did the Lord prepare something for them to eat. Since he loved them, why did he allow them to spend that time in hard labour? Couldn't he have prepared the loaves and fish beforehand or couldn't he have informed them beforehand that he had made provision for them to have a meal, so that they need not have laboured all night?

That was not the course he chose. He did not want his disciples to be lazy people. Although they failed to obtain anything, they diligently did their duty and it was only afterwards that the Lord prepared something for them to eat. Had they been lazy and spent the time sleeping, he would have taken no responsibility for them. So long as we do our work diligently and faithfully carry out our duties, the Lord will certainly come to our aid. But if we are unwilling to work diligently, he will allow us to go hungry.

It is true that we ought not to be troubled and anxious in regard to the question of what we eat, but that does not mean that we should do other than work as hard as we can. (19)

One thing God has spoken, two things have I heard: that you, O God, are strong, and that you, O Lord, are loving.
Psalm 62:11, 12

'You, O God, are strong.' What a precious truth! The servants of God who are engaged in propagating the gospel need power. It requires power to arouse believers who have fallen into a deep sleep; to nurture and to guide the flock of God; to combat our spiritual enemies. It requires even more power to deal with all kinds of trouble and to handle various undertakings.

Where power is lacking, the servants of God are severely restricted: they can never serve as guides; they can never achieve success; they can never forge ahead; they can never be victorious.

The secret of obtaining power from God is not to force the pace but quietly to wait. For 'he gives strength to the weary and increases the power of the weak. Even youths grow tired and weary, and young men stumble and fall; but those who hope in the Lord will renew their strength. They will soar on wings like eagles; they will run and not grow weary, they will walk and not be faint' (Isaiah 40:29–31). (7)

Joseph said to them, 'Don't be afraid. Am I in the place of God? You intended to harm me, but God intended it for good to accomplish what is now being done, the saving of many lives.'　　　　　　**Genesis 50:19, 20**

Joseph did not regard his brothers as enemies who were plotting to harm him. He regarded them as instruments that God was using to carry out his purposes.

So long as we maintain an attitude of worship and sincerity in the sight of God, and so long as we do the will of God, God will bless us through those who hate us, just as he blesses us through those who love us. Evil men may plot to harm us; they may attack us and do us injury; but all these things can become the smelting furnaces that God uses in refining away our dross.

There are many lessons to be learned in life, and if no hostility were ever to come our way, we might never have the opportunity to learn some of these. When under attack, we inevitably feel that we are unfortunate and that we are being wronged. But when the time comes for all things to be manifested – and not till then – we shall understand that the good we experience through the instrumentality of those who are hostile to us, may not be a whit less than the good we experience through friends. The time will certainly come when we shall say to them: 'You intended to harm me, but God intended it for good.' (19)

They took Jonah and threw him overboard, and the raging sea grew calm.   Jonah 1:15

Sometimes our lives seem to be like the sea when a violent storm arises and the waves get rougher and rougher (Jonah 1:4, 11).

If we call upon God sincerely, he will indicate to us whatever it is in the ship of our lives that has provoked his wrath. Covetousness, pride, envy, hatred, deceit, self-seeking, slander, licentiousness – if only *one* of these sins is cherished in our lives it is enough to create turbulence like the wind and the waves. So danger arises and we lose our peace and joy and power.

Fellow-believers! I speak to you whose hearts are in the grip of suffering and you who have lost your peace! Why not ask God to show you what, after all, is the 'Jonah' in your ship? As soon as you have the answer, let no soft-heartedness deter you from getting hold of him and casting him into the sea. 'He' may be a sin in thought, word or deed or a tainted possession. As soon as God enlightens you, then waste no time in dealing with or getting rid of whatever it is. (19)

O Lord our God, you answered them; you were to Israel a forgiving God, though you punished their misdeeds.
          Psalm 99:8

He will not always accuse, nor will he harbour his anger for ever; he does not treat us as our sins deserve or repay us according to our iniquities.   **Psalm 103:9, 10**

The fact that God forgives our sins is because he loves us; that he punishes us according to our misdeeds is also because he loves us. That God forgives our sins is for our good; that he punishes us according to what we have done is also for our good.

When we repent and confess our sins, we may only ask God to forgive us for those sins; we may not ask him to take away the punishment and suffering that rightly come to us; or rather, we should not demandingly make such a request. When God sees that what we pray for is for our good and exacts no further retribution, we joyfully accept this as an act of grace. But if, on the other hand, God sees that for us to suffer for what we have done is even more for our good and so punishes us even after forgiving us, we still ought to adopt an attitude of thanksgiving and obedience and receive what he has appointed for us.

So long as we are willing to allow God to treat us according to his good and acceptable will and don't grumble or act stubbornly, we shall certainly be able to perceive that what he does for us is many times better and many times higher than what we ourselves could have imagined. (19)

I have brought you glory on earth by completing the work you gave me to do.   **John 17:4**

In the eyes of men, 'success' often refers to the successful accomplishment of major projects. But in the eyes of the Lord Jesus, the way to bring glory to God was to complete the work that God had given him to do – that and only that being true success.

There are indeed some Christians who, either in the church or in society, have great achievements to their credit and, as a consequence, are admired by many people and have attained a high standing. Yet they have not glorified God for they have not done the work that God gave them to do. In the sight of men, they are successful but in the eyes of God, they are failures.

However, there are other Christians who, in this matter, are like their Lord. They do not shout or cry out or raise their voice in the streets (Isaiah 42:2). They are also like the Lord Jesus in being despised and rejected by men, a man of sorrows and familiar with suffering (Isaiah 53). These Christians are glorifying God through their holy and upright lives. They are striving with all their heart and strength to do the things that God gave them to do. They may not receive any praise from men but they receive the praise of God. (14)

After the people saw the miraculous sign that Jesus did, they began to say: 'Surely this is the Prophet who is to come into the world.' Jesus, knowing that they intended to come and make him king by force, withdrew again into the hills by himself.   **John 6:14, 15**

In view of the fact that when Christians achieve something notable they almost inevitably face this kind of temptation, we must ask ourselves whether there is a way of escaping this danger. The answer is, 'Yes!'

The secret is to do what the Lord Jesus did. After he had completed a particular task, he retired as quickly as he could to the hills where he could be alone and pray.

We too ought, invariably, to seek a quiet place where we can be alone to communicate with God. We should ask God to prevent us from falling into the snare of the devil; to keep us from becoming proud as a result of being exalted and praised by other people; to keep us from becoming covetous of the possessions and advantages and riches lying before us; to keep us from becoming lovers of the world as a result of increasing possessions; and to keep us from becoming dissolute as a result of favourable circumstances.

After we have been used to accomplish any work of importance, we should do that which I have just advocated without delay. To delay even a little is enough to allow the devil to force his way in and to assume control. In such an event, the repercussions do not bear imagining. (14)

**(Jesus) said to him, 'Zacchaeus, come down immedi-
ately. I must stay at your house today.'**   Luke 19:5

Why are we unwilling to go to the home of sinners? The first
reason is pride. If we look at ourselves from God's viewpoint
then we shall lose all excuse for being proud, and in no
circumstances can we despise even the vilest of sinners. If
anyone at all has the right to look down on sinners, to criticise
or condemn them, it is the Lord Jesus and him alone. For he
alone never fell into sin, nor at any time was deceit found in
his mouth. Yet he did not despise sinners nor criticise them.
Still less did he condemn them. On the contrary, he went
everywhere seeking for lost sinners; with all his heart and
strength, he sought to save them.

If our Lord – the holy and sinless Jesus – was like this, what
grounds have we for being different? Our own hearts were
originally defiled (Jeremiah 17:9); we fell into sin and we had
no means of saving ourselves; in fact, we were no different
from all other sinners. But, through the love and compassion
of God and the salvation of the Lord Jesus Christ, we have
attained our present position. So how much more ought we to
show our compassion and sympathy to all those sinners who
have not yet received what we have! (14)

All the people . . . began to mutter, 'He has gone to be the guest of a "sinner".'   **Luke 19:7**

We should reprove and appeal to those who have sunk deeply into the pit of sin and have not yet awakened to their need.

But as for those who are ashamed of their sin and who grieve over their sin – having tried unsuccessfully to extricate themselves from its grip – we must consistently respect them and have compassion on them. We must not lose contact with them; we must do all that we can to help them. When we hear certain people being described as depraved or when we perceive elements of wickedness in their conduct, we should on no account adopt a derogatory attitude towards them. We should avoid becoming bitter towards them; we certainly shouldn't avoid associating with them merely on the grounds of our becoming the objects of criticism, for then we would be abandoning the very people who need help and compassion.

O Lord! Fill my heart with your great love and enable me to live like you in showing sympathy for people and having compassion on them. Enable me also to be like you in ever working diligently and in being ready at any time to travel anywhere in order to seek and save the lost. Enable me also not to be afraid of being despised, misunderstood and criticised or being called the friend of taxgatherers and sinners on account of my love for you. (14)

Month 6: Day 18 — No immunity from pain

I have been blameless before him and have kept myself from sin. The Lord has rewarded me according to my righteousness, according to the cleanness of my hands in his sight. Psalm 18:23, 24

You have perhaps been living a life of obedience to God and engaged in doing good; yet, contrary to your expectation, you have been misunderstood and even vilified. Does this disappoint you? Does it make you backslide? Open your Bible and consider the experiences of the saints of old. How many were immune from bitter and intolerable circumstances? When the brave and faithful King David attacked the enemy and delivered the people, he was not only unrewarded but also pursued everywhere by the evil King Saul – a man who was envious of the worthy. David had no home to return to and he had to endure all kinds of suffering, but never did he contend for himself. On two occasions, God delivered his enemy into his hand yet he refrained from taking his revenge and made no move to vindicate himself. But when God's time had come, he not only vindicated David but also specially comforted and rewarded him for all the suffering and wrong that he had endured.

Didn't the prophets in the Old Testament and apostles in the New Testament also suffer many wrongs that were never redressed? They gave up occupation, pleasures, money and fame in order to save people. Logically everyone should have thanked and loved them but, contrary to all reason, the people not only failed to treat them in this way but also misunderstood, vilified and attacked them or, even, put them to death. (19)

He was oppressed and afflicted, yet he did not open his mouth; he was led like a lamb to the slaughter, and as a sheep before her shearers is silent, so he did not open his mouth.　　　　　　　　　　　　　　　**Isaiah 53:7**

When we turn to the Lord Jesus Christ, the Son of God, and recall all that he had to face, it's very disturbing.

Consider what he did. He gave up the glory of heaven; he humbled himself and became the Son of Man; he willingly became poor and lowly – all in order that he might carry out the great work of saving people.

Not only did he find himself unwelcomed in the world but also he was despised, rejected, opposed and persecuted. Even this failed to satisfy the people and they finally crucified him. When Roman soldiers nailed him to the cross, he did not contend for himself; when passers-by shook their heads and ridiculed him, he did not contend for himself; even when the robber who was crucified with him reviled him, he still did not contend for himself. He was aware that to contend for himself was counter-productive; even more was he aware that the righteous God would contend on his behalf. So he endured all these things in silence.

When the time came, God *did* contend for him. 'God exalted him to the highest place and gave him the name that is above every name, that at the name of Jesus every knee should bow, in heaven and on earth and under the earth, and every tongue confess that Jesus Christ is Lord, to the glory of God the Father' (Philippians 2:9–11). (19)

Jesus . . . said, 'Go home to your family and tell them
how much the Lord has done for you, and how he has
had mercy on you.'   Mark 5:19

The gifts that we variously receive are different from each
other. Not all Christians are equipped to preach the word to
people or even to talk about the word to people. But should
that be a hindrance? Shouldn't we all do what we are able to
do? Those who are able to preach should preach and those
who are able to talk to people about the gospel should do so.

  Those who cannot do either of these things, should first of
all undertake a ministry of prayer both for the preachers and
also for the hearers. They may also take people with them to
meetings where they can hear the gospel and they can pass on
evangelistic literature and other good literature to their
friends.

  Apart from all these activities, there is one very important
ministry that every disciple of the Lord is able to do and
ought to do. It is this: 'Go home to your family and tell them
how much the Lord has done for you, and how he has had
mercy on you.'

  In addition to this, what God wants even more is that
through your manner of life and your holy character after
your conversion, you demonstrate that your testimony is
true. If all who belonged to the Lord would act in this way,
then undoubtedly there would be far more people turning to
the Lord than there are at present.

  Beloved fellow-believers! Have you today appreciated
your responsibilities? (7)

I urge you, brothers, in view of God's mercy, to offer your bodies as living sacrifices, holy and pleasing to God – which is your spiritual worship.   Romans 12:1, 2

Being wholly consecrated to God does not necessarily involve having a full-time preaching ministry. Obviously, Christians who are full-time preachers must first be wholly consecrated to God but Christians who are fully consecrated to God are not obliged to become full-time preachers. Everyone who has been saved by grace ought to be wholly consecrated to God but only the few who are specially sent by God to be full-time preachers should be doing this work.

To be fully consecrated means to place yourself in the hands of God. You no longer belong to yourself; you belong to God. This means that in no respect are you the master; you allow only God to be master. The road that you follow is the one that God commands you to follow; the work that you undertake is the work that he directs you to undertake. Your location is where the Lord places you. You no longer make the choice; you no longer make the plans; you no longer decide on the arrangements. Those who are consecrated to God no longer have a choice; all that remains for them is to obey.

If you say, 'I have made up my mind to become a full-time preacher and not to do anything else,' that attitude is sufficient to demonstrate that you have not yet wholly consecrated yourself to God. For one who is wholly consecrated to God should not be talking in this fashion. (16)

Demas, because he loved this world, has deserted me and has gone to Thessalonica. Crescens has gone to Galatia, and Titus to Dalmatia.   **2 Timothy 4:10**

Aren't there many people like Demas in the church today? To begin with they zealously follow Jesus and regard everything as loss compared with the knowledge of him. But after a few months or years, they desert the Lord through love of the world and go off elsewhere.

Fellow-disciples of Christ! You need to watch. Do not allow love for the world to grow up within you! There is no foothold for a Christian in the world and there ought to be no foothold for the world in a Christian. It is not possible for a Christian to hold Christ in one hand and the world in the other. If it is not a case of loosening our grip to let the world go, then it is a case of loosening our grip to let Christ go. If you loosen your grip of the world in order to follow Christ, you will be rewarded with lasting satisfaction. But if you loosen your grip of Christ through love of the world, you will suffer loss beyond description.

I would ask you: which is trivial and which is important? Which will you get rid of and which will you retain? You must be extremely watchful. 'Demas, because he loved this world, has deserted me and gone to Thessalonica.' When I first read this statement I was sad for Paul. Then I pitied Demas. But I ended up by being fearful for myself. (12)

Better is open rebuke than hidden love. The kisses of an enemy may be profuse, but faithful are the wounds of a friend.   **Proverbs 27:5, 6**

We may not be well placed to perceive our own shortcomings and failings. But these may be perceived by the people around us very plainly. In the same way, other people may not perceive their own shortcomings and failings while we as onlookers may see them very plainly.

This makes it necessary that there should be mutual reproof and admonition. No matter how concerned you are about other believers, if you observe their faults and yet refrain from reproving and admonishing them, your love for them is less than perfect and you are neglecting a major duty.

If you neglect this duty, the consequences will be two-fold. On the one hand, the transgressors will not be perfect before God and, on the other, their transgressions will bring them affliction and suffering. Also, through their transgressions, other people will suffer harm and the name of God will be dishonoured. (16)

Better is open rebuke than hidden love. The kisses of an enemy may be profuse, but faithful are the wounds of a friend.   **Proverbs 27:5, 6**

There are times when the rebukes and admonitions directed to us by other people are based on incorrect observation or on unsubstantiated rumours; times when we are, in fact, quite innocent of the faults of which we are accused.

How should we act when we encounter such circumstances? Naturally, we should not resort to telling untruths and confess to having faults that we do not have. On the other hand, we should not become angry with those who rebuke and admonish us acting on incorrect information. Even though we cannot accept their rebukes and admonition, we can certainly accept the love that lies behind their action. So we ought, first, to express our thanks to those involved for their loving concern and only then to state clearly the true situation as persuasively as we can.

If we respond in this way, then those who reprove and admonish us will surely deeply admire us and, what is more, still be prepared to reprove and admonish us in the future as they have done in the past.

If, on the other hand, we respond angrily to those who have admonished us, they might indeed apologise and acknowledge that they have misunderstood us, but wouldn't they be too embarrassed to reprove and admonish us again? If so, we'd be forfeiting their help for a long time to come. (16)

Better is open rebuke than hidden love. The kisses of an enemy may be profuse, but faithful are the wounds of a friend.   **Proverbs 27:5, 6**

To reprove and admonish other people not only requires love, it also requires courage. For there are very few people who willingly accept reproof and admonition. Most people are only too happy to accept commendation and praise but dislike rebuke and admonition. They think that for people to speak of their faults is but to shame them and do harm to them.

Not only unbelievers but also true believers are among those who adopt such an attitude. Some believers wholeheartedly aspire to a holy life and set themselves to get rid of their faults and shortcomings but when other people reprove and admonish them, they feel uncomfortable.

Being aware of this situation, we are conscious of difficulty. On the one hand, we fear to give offence and, on the other hand, we fear to cause embarrassment. With these two anxieties, we find ourselves in a quandary. We are constrained to speak but we refrain from doing so.

If we want to please God and help other believers, we must overcome our diffidence and, when we observe the faults of our brothers and sisters, take our courage in both hands and admonish them. (16)

**Blessed is he whose transgressions are forgiven, whose
sins are covered.**   **Psalm 32:1**

**Therefore confess your sins to each other and pray for
each other so that you may be healed. The prayer of a
righteous man is powerful and effective.**   **James 5:16**

'Confess your sins to each other.' For many believers this is
an extremely difficult exercise since it means that we are
brought very low. It necessitates subduing one's pride,
denying oneself and bending low before other people.

Those who love vainglory are unwilling to confess their
sins to other people; those who are proud and arrogant are
unwilling to confess their sins to other people; those who
regard themselves as in the right are unwilling to confess
their sins to other people. In their eyes such confession is a
matter of shame, of lowering ranks and of losing 'face.'

Many people have done wrong and injured other people
and in their hearts they recognise that they have sinned. But
they are unwilling to confess with their mouth that they have
been at fault. Yet out of all the people in the world, who is
there without fault? To have a fault and yet be willing to
confess it, is truly a mark of sincerity. It is also something to
be respected and admired. We must not regard the confession of faults as something to be ashamed of; indeed we
must regard it as a matter of glory. It is shameful, rather, to
refrain from confessing our faults. We should strive to learn
to be willing to confess our faults; we should dare to confess
our faults. (19)

Blessed is he whose transgressions are forgiven, whose sins are covered.   **Psalm 32:1**

Therefore confess your sins to each other and pray for each other so that you may be healed. The prayer of a righteous man is powerful and effective.   **James 5:16**

Who ought first to acknowledge his sins? Logically speaking, those who first sinned ought to be first in acknowledging their sins. Yet in practice this isn't always the way. The correct track to follow is this: Whoever is first reproved by the Spirit ought to be first in acknowledging his sin. Whenever it is a case of sharing some benefit, you should allow other people to go ahead of you. But when it is a case of acknowledging sin, then you should take the lead.

Whoever first acknowledges his sin is the one who first obtains the blessing. Whoever first acknowledges his sin is the one who is great. Whoever first acknowledges his sin is the one who is victorious.

Suppose I become involved in a quarrel with another believer. I am well aware that it was he who began the quarrel and yet I myself am not without sin. As soon as I am enlightened by God, I ought to confess my sin to him. This action on my part may influence him to confess his own sin. Even if he is not moved and refuses to acknowledge his sin, yet in the sight of God I would have done all that I could and I would certainly receive from God the blessing that he bestows.

Once we understand that acknowledging one's sin is the path to blessing, then we shall be contenders to be first in acknowledging our sin.

Beloved reader! Are you willing to try out this way? (19)

Month 6: Day 28   Menders needed

**If you spend yourselves on behalf of the hungry and
satisfy the needs of the oppressed, then your light will
rise in the darkness, and your night will become like the
noonday. The Lord will guide you always; he will
satisfy your needs in a sun-scorched land and will
strengthen your frame. You will be like a well-watered
garden, like a spring whose waters never fail. Your
people will rebuild the ancient ruins and will raise up
the age-old foundations; you will be called Repairer of
Broken Walls, Restorer of Streets with Dwellings.**

                                        Isaiah 58:10–12

In order to be one who repairs broken walls you must be free
from broken walls yourself. Only those who abandon their
sin and who do the will of God are pleasing to him. Only
when they do this will the prayers that they offer up either for
themselves or for others be heard by God.

Had Moses not been a man who did the will of God and
who had done the things that pleased God, God would on no
account have listened to his plea and acted leniently towards
the rebellious Israelites. Had Moses not been one who
forsook his sins, as if they were enemies, he could not have
given vent to his fierce anger on account of the people's
transgressions nor could he have reproved and punished
them. And in this case, he could not have stopped the breach
for them.

Those who are to stop breaches, to repair and restore,
must have authority before God, so that he will listen to their
prayers, and they must have authority before men, so that
they will stand in awe of them and have a healthy fear of their
rebuke. Only those who abandon their sin and do the will of
God possess authority like this. (16)

You of little faith . . . why did you doubt?

Matthew 14:31

These words of rebuke, addressed by the Lord to Peter
(Matthew 14:22–33), are to be seen as words of rebuke to us.

When our eyes are wholly on the Lord, although the
outward circumstances are terrifying and make us tremble,
just like turbulent seas, we take no notice of them. For the
peace bestowed by the Lord is in our hearts. Our life is a life
of victory, as the Lord's was. Just like the Lord – in a sense –
we may walk on water without sinking.

But when we cease to keep our eyes on the Lord and look
instead at our frightening environment, we become alarmed
and lose our heads. We are about to sink into all those things
that frighten us and accumulate in our hearts – anxiety, grief,
despair, timidity, doubt, apprehension. Our life undergoes
an immediate change. We feel that we shall not again walk on
the water – in fact we have already begun to sink.

In these circumstances, if we do not cry without delay,
'Lord, save me!' we truly do not know to what pitiable state
we are capable of falling. (19)

Jesus was in the stern, sleeping on a cushion . . . He got up, rebuked the wind and said to the waves, 'Quiet! Be still!'   **Mark 4:38, 39**

Fellow Christian disciples! Don't be afraid! Don't give way to trembling! So long as the Lord is with us, no matter how fierce the wind, no matter how strong the waves, nothing can harm even a hair of our heads (Mark 4:35–41). Although he permits the winds and the waves to buffet us constantly, and although there are times when he appears to be asleep and totally unconcerned about us, it is all in accordance with his perfect will. He wants to use these things to test our faith so that we can appreciate afresh his almighty power and thus learn to trust him more.

The world in which we live is truly like a vast ocean and every day of our life is as if we were sailing in a skiff on the surface of that ocean. What is necessary is to remember that our Lord is sailing with us in the boat and that he is always at our side. It is even more necessary that we should remember that he is the Lord who overcame the world – the one who holds all authority in heaven and earth. So no matter how fierce the wind and how violent the waves, we can always remain unruffled in tranquillity and safety, undisturbed by fear. After he has commanded the wind and the waves to be still, we can then reverently bow before him in worship and say, 'This is indeed the Lord. Even the wind and waves obey him!' (19)